Drama Activities for K–6 Students

Creating Classroom Spirit

Milton E. Polsky
Dorothy Napp Schindel
Carmine Tabone

Rowman & Littlefield Education
Lanham, Maryland • Toronto • Oxford
2006

Published in the United States of America
by Rowman & Littlefield Education
A Division of Rowman & Littlefield Publishers, Inc.
A wholly owned subsidiary of The Rowman & Littlefield Publishing Group, Inc.
4501 Forbes Boulevard, Suite 200, Lanham, Maryland 20706
www.rowmaneducation.com

PO Box 317
Oxford
OX2 9RU, UK

British Library Cataloguing in Publication Information Available

Library of Congress Cataloging-in-Publication Data

Polsky, Milton E.
  Drama activities for K–6 students : creating classroom spirit / Milton E. Polsky,
Dorothy Napp Schindel, Carmine Tabone.
      p. cm.
  Includes bibliographical references.
  ISBN-13: 978-1-57886-444-7 (hardcover : alk. paper)
  ISBN-10: 1-57886-444-5 (hardcover : alk. paper)
  ISBN-13: 978-1-57886-445-4 (pbk. : alk. paper)
  ISBN-10: 1-57886-445-3 (pbk. : alk. paper)
  1. Drama in education. 2. Theater—Study and teaching (Elementary) I. Schindel,
Dorothy Napp, 1942– II. Tabone, Carmine, 1946– III. Title.
  PN3171.P57 2006
  372.139'9—dc22
                                                                    2006006499

⊗™ The paper used in this publication meets the minimum requirements of
American National Standard for Information Sciences—Permanence of
Paper for Printed Library Materials, ANSI/NISO Z39.48-1992.
Manufactured in the United States of America.

Dedicated to the memory of
Nellie McCaslin and Lowell Swortzell,
who touched our lives, and the lives of children,
with drama

I dream a world where man
No other man will scorn,
Where love will bless the earth
And peace its path adorn.
I dream a world where all
Will know sweet freedom's way . . .

From "I Dream a World," by Langston Hughes

CONTENTS

CONTENTS

ACKNOWLEDGMENTS

We wish to acknowledge the creative efforts of the young people and their teachers with whom we have worked through the years. They have been the inspiration for our work and, indeed, for this book. Thank you. Milton wishes to specifically thank the PS 50, PS 183 After-School Program, and PS 20 Manhattan communities, where he wrote and developed the Skywoman creation story, "The Friendly Forest," "The Curse of the Water Monster Creature," "Rosa Parks Responds With Pride," and the Sadako and "We Still Have a Dream" scenarios. He thanks the children in the kindergarten class of his wife, Roberta, and Elizabeth Rosen's third-grade class at PS 20 in New York City. He thanks Howard Berland for feedback on the poetry in the book and Sally-Anne Milgrim for perceptive editorial assistance. Dorothy would like to thank Lynne J. Foster, her original Acting Through Art collaborator, and her former students and colleagues at Packer Collegiate Institute, Brooklyn Heights, New York, where her work on "Swimmy" and "Duck in the Gun" began and where her peace education projects were encouraged, developed, nurtured, and then "taken on the road." Dorothy gives special thanks to David Stein and the Giannini and Carlson families for their time and help and to her DramaMUSE partner Jennifer Fell Hayes for continual collaboration and inspiration. Carmine would like to thank all the members of the Educational Arts Team for their support and creativity: Mary Aiken, Robert Albrecht, Roxanne Arrojo, Dina Bruno, Dom Buccafusco, Kelly Darr, Peter La Brusciano, Sobha Paredes, Carlos

ACKNOWLEDGMENTS

Ponton, Paul Sanabria, and Lorenzo Veguilla. We wish to acknowledge our families for their enthusiasm, patience, devotion, and help on this project. Infinite gratitude goes to Roberta Polsky, Stephen Schindel, and Laura Tabone and to our children and our grandchildren. May you all grow up in a peaceful and loving world. We wish to acknowledge our quote from "I Dream a World" from the *Collected Poems of Langston Hughes*, by Langston Hughes, copyright © 1994 by the Estate of Langston Hughes. Used by permission of Alfred A. Knopf, a division of Random House, Inc. And finally, we thank our editors at Rowman & Littlefield Education, Niki Guinan, Paul Cacciato, and Cindy Tursman, for their generous help.

FOREWORD

In this valuable new book, the authors, accomplished arts educators, have provided ways to guide children to understand the creative process by actively participating in dramatic activities that expose them to the art of drama and that, just as significant, impinge on other areas of their learning.

It has long been known that children's awareness of the meaning of both the written and the spoken word is best awakened through dramatic activities emphasizing body language, gestures, and movement. The intent of the artist whose works are being examined, as well as the ability of children to interpret this intent through their own creative work, is another vital outcome of such activities.

As a musician and music educator, I strongly believe that songs and other musical forms—the tone poem, program music, for example—are best understood and even best performed by the world's greatest artists through an understanding of the text. In a recent interview, the virtually perfect soprano Renée Fleming was asked if she had a favorite aria. Her reply was "Song to the Moon" from the Dvorak opera *Rusalka*. One need only listen and watch her performance to see, immediately, the inextricable connection between text, melody, and dramatic gesture in her matchless interpretation.

So it is with all who seek to learn about stories and enter the world of artist in order to apprehend what it is he or she is trying to communicate. "Acting out the story," which is really the basis of this book, produces young people who become attuned to the creative process and, through that participatory strategy, become artists themselves. Further, as the authors point out, the very act of engaging in dramatic activities results in a "spirit of teamwork and cooperation" at its best. Educators are certainly familiar with the concept of "cooperative learning," but engaging each other through the arts raises children to the highest level of sharing thoughts and ideas.

Lately in education, the need to enhance children's ability to care about one another has become a long-overdue goal for the classroom (it has also become a necessary outcome in the preparation of teachers). But in few instances within texts designed for teachers are there actual suggestions for creating the caring classroom. This book does it.

Dealing with feelings, the desirable end of dramatic activities, leads children to a full and deep understanding of themselves. This is accomplished through a nonthreatening—indeed, celebratory—classroom atmosphere generated when the children are encouraged to express their emotions by acting out those of the author, poet, artist through characterization or visual statement. The splendid result is that they learn how everyone reacts to events and ideas with which we are surrounded every day and in every society.

Another contribution of this book is that the approach to creating such a classroom, to reaching the hearts and minds of all children, is that all teachers can find in it seemingly endless ways to introduce their classes to the beauty of drama in story, poem, play, and picture. Moreover, the outlines of actual lesson plans designed for the novice at this sort of activity, as well as for those who are more experienced in the arts and in translating aesthetic feelings into their own lives and the lives of others, are clearly presented and well organized, containing step-by-step suggestions for how to proceed.

The result is that children, with only minimal guidance from the teacher, work out the dramatization—the "choreography" as it were—to blend thoughts, feelings, and textual understandings. This is not a teacher-dominated activity, because it so closely parallels the rules of engagement in the artistic process. That these activities clearly articulate these rules is important for the teacher because they also hold the key to teaching children to read, thereby improving their literacy skills. The activities guide children to react to ideas that form the basis for the social studies that deal with the history, times, and events surrounding the creation of works of art by mature artists, and they lead the children to create in similar fashion.

It is refreshing to read a text of which the basis is an age-old belief in the power of the arts to release the imagination of children, coupled with content that is superbly chosen for its relevance to their needs in today's world.

Jerrold Ross, Dean
School of Education, St. John's University, New York City

INTRODUCTION

Welcome to the world of creative drama and playmaking! The goal of this book is to share with you exciting ways to guide students to improvise plays based on poems, stories, and pictures with peace-related themes. We believe a peacefully creative classroom promotes the spirit of teamwork, requiring a high degree of cooperation, caring, and the communication of feelings. The poems and stories that we have selected are themselves about cooperation and caring as well as about everyday problems and conflicts that need to be resolved if people are to live in harmony.

Along the way, students will become people and animals who sometimes help each other and sometimes get in each other's way. Most learn how to reach meaningful compromises, whereas others provide examples of what can happen when their negative actions go unaddressed. The students' enactments of these characters will take children to different lands around the globe, back into time, and into their own neighborhoods. The students will enjoy taking their imaginative journeys on the wings of such varied theatrical forms as pantomime plays, shadow theater, living newspaper, story theater, and creative tableaus. In many of the dramatizations, teachers can also play a role.

To help students create their own variations of the stories with their own dialogue, we provide easy-to-follow structures. Within a framework of warm-up, development, and wrap-up, you and your students will discover challenging inquiry and writing techniques and participate in mind-opening discussions and enrichments that can be applied across the curriculum. All the activities are designed to promote a deep sense of trust, mutual respect, and pride in working together.

Let the journeys begin!

CHAPTER ONE
GETTING STARTED

Before you embark on any creative drama project, you will find it a good idea to pick out a story that you think your students will enjoy acting out. We have provided stories that deal with important issues of working together cooperatively in an atmosphere that encourages peaceful action and reflection. Make sure that you have clear goals for the enactment and that your objectives are doable within a realistic time frame. Some sessions will span a number of periods. You know best. We have provided structures for warm-up, development, and wrap-up that will help you to realize your goals in ways that engage the students. Feel free to personalize the plans so that they become custom-made to best fit the needs of you and your students.

Creative drama involves activities comprising the imaginative use of body and voice. From time to time in this book, we suggest using useful materials, such as pictures, for both the warm-up and the development parts of the sessions. We also provide some ideas for creative costumes and scenery, if you decide to present more advanced story dramatizations for invited audiences.

The essence of drama in any form is human conflict and the expression of many varied feelings. The irony of working with drama is that students, to discover and imaginatively resolve confrontation, must work together, create together, and through this process learn from each other. Good luck with your program as you start on your peaceful and spirited journey in creative drama.

Guiding Students to Work in Groups

Positive group interaction is vital when creating plays in the classroom. In classroom drama work, there are basically two kinds of groups: the entire class working as a whole and the class divided into subgroups of two to five students working on different parts of the play or on different versions of the same play. As you will see in our lesson plans, the entire class, regardless of age, first engages in primary questioning, discussion, and brainstorming. Then older students (Grades 3 and up) may be asked to work in subgroups, creating drama that they will share in some way with the class as a whole.

Here are six suggestions for keeping the creative juices flowing in an atmosphere that promotes an imaginative give-and-take of ideas and feelings.

Start With a Circle Formation

Working in a circle places participants on equal footing. There is no beginning or end in a circle, a configuration that promotes unity and teamwork. Because there are no corners in a circle, everyone can see each other and listen to each other's ideas. Always keep in mind age appropriateness when forming a circle. For example, young students (K–2) can sit on the floor, preferably on a designated piece of rug or carpet. Older students (starting with Grade 3) do best sitting in chairs. If you conduct your drama classes in a gym or comparable setting, older students may wish to sit on the floor or use a combination of the floor and chairs.

Maintain Control and Focus

Of course, the best way to keep students attentive and involved in creative drama, which requires all-out concentration, is through telling, inquiring about, and enacting an exciting story or poem. These techniques work especially well for maintaining student focus:

> *Teacher-in-role:* In drama work, students are more likely to come up with creative contributions if they are encouraged to re-

spond to you as a character than to you as a teacher. For example, while telling a story, you can adjust its pacing and rhythm. *The king asked everyone to take a deep breath and rest a second. "Quiet, please, I say to thee."* You can ask questions in role, for example, as a news reporter interviewing the Three Pigs.

The magic drum: A drum and mallet or a coffee can with stick can be an invaluable tool for getting attention and signaling the need to stop. Practice by asking students to make a sound and then, with a drumbeat, to stop all at once so that they can hear and appreciate the silence. Keep repeating the exercise until everyone stops precisely at the same moment or second. You can also practice this technique with students by asking them to move, move, move, take a shape, and then freeze to stone.

Peace words: You can work with your class to devise some special words and movements that are signals to stop, look, and listen—for example, *Peace freeze, Stop,* and *Silence, everyone.* Keep these phrases short and doable. The sooner that participants can be silent to receive instructions, the more creative pleasure everyone will enjoy.

Helping young people practice self-control—hand signals and "Freeze to stone!" (Photo: Roberta Polsky)

Elicit Ideas for Enactment

Our lesson plans offer ample suggestions for story starters and ways for students to get into the stories and their interpretations. Here are some general pointers:

- Emphasize the need for everyone to talk one at a time, to listen to each other, and to be respectful of each other's ideas and feelings.

- Ask students to raise their hands, hold them still, and softly call out "Idea." Then proceed to call on whomever you wish. In cases where there is a flurry of responses and many hands are held high, quickly assign a speaking order.

- Tie ideas together, or students can do so if they are working in subgroups, through brainstorming until one idea emerges that works. Ask questions and encourage students to ask them (see Ten Things for Young People to Practice, pp. 6–7), for example, Did the group show imagination? Specifically, how? Did the group show teamwork? Specifically, how? Sometimes, the unexpected works. Use it! Keep clarity and interest in mind. As Goethe said, "When interest lags, so does memory."

Side Coach to Develop Ideas

It is such a wonderful feeling when students begin to develop their dramatic ideas. Sometimes the group as a whole will contribute ideas that everyone can share and develop. At other times leaders will emerge to guide their classmates in small groups.

- Encourage student-centered work by literally stepping behind or away from the circle, whole-class involvement, or subgroup work so that students can feel that the ideas are emanating from them, not you. Fan their creative sparks by asking questions that focus their inquiry into fleshing out the characters.

- Practice with students ways to address their ideas to each other and engage in interactive discussion.

- Use the "teacher-in-role" technique whenever it is appropriate and nonobtrusive. For example, though there may not be a messenger in the story, you can be one, asking the queen important information that advances the story.

Count Off Students Into Small Groups

When it comes time to form subgroups, think about the various ways that you might do so. You can form little subgroups, even students in pairs, within the circle—for example, groups of four linking their arms to become instant spiders. The following suggestions are for students, starting with Grade 3.

- You may wish to place specific students together, keep certain students apart, or ask for volunteers to make up a subgroup.

- You may wish to choose captains, who in turn each pick a student, who in turn choose another. This process is called *making microgroups*, usually consisting of participants who work well together.

- You may wish to count off groups. Go around the circle saying, "One, two, three, . . . " (the number of groups you want), asking all the ones to go to one part of the room, the twos to go to another part, and so on. This is called *randomization*, which is a great way for ensuring a mix of different students to work cooperatively together.

Create a Work/Share Space

After working in their designated areas, students can, of course, share their work in a number of exciting settings not limited to performing in front of the class. For example, as they go off to their own areas of the room, they can both create their scenes and perform them in this chosen space with the audience (fellow classmates) moving to and around them. This procedure places emphasis on process and sharing rather than on performing up front. In addition, the perception is that the group is working in a play space rather than on a stage. Another important factor is that for the sharing, any needed props, costume pieces, and scenic elements can be set up in one spot so that nothing has to be moved for sharing the work.

Another venue is to take the scene or play to different classrooms as part of a traveling "creative caravan." Use dialogue and pantomime or simple props to convey the essence of the dramatic piece. Choose student directors, stage managers, and crew to get it all together. Keep your options open, because students enjoy a spontaneous activity as long as it is grounded on a firm structure. As Louis Pasteur observed, "Chance favors the prepared mind." Enjoy!

Ten Things for Young People to Practice

Share these suggestions with your students. Feel free to make changes. Add your own.

Planning

1. Listen carefully to each other.

2. Talk one at a time. You'll get more done.

3. Be respectful of each other's ideas and feelings.

4. Say "Here's another idea" instead of "My idea is better."

5. Tie ideas together until you have one that works.

6. Be prepared to do some parts over if they are not clear.

Revising

7. Ask questions like these:
   - Did the group show imagination? Specifically, how?
   - Did the group show teamwork? Specifically, how?
   - Did the group show the feelings of the characters? Specifically, how?

8. Expect the unexpected. If something works, use it. Revise for clarity and interest.

9. Focus on what you're trying to accomplish. Remember your goals. Keep a clear framework of how you will do it. Go with the flow and energy of the group.

10. Listen to each other, support each other, and enjoy each other's efforts.

How to Transform Stories Into Plays With Students (Grades K–2)

In this creative drama method, the whole group at the same time acts out the story while it is being told by the teacher/leader or by one of the students. Make sure that you have a goal in mind or one written down and any materials that you will need for acting out the story.

Warm-Up

1. Start by having the students sit in a circle formation.

2. Motivate them by connecting the story with their interests and experiences. For example, if the story is "The Animals Help Skywoman Create the World: Native American Creation Myth" (see pp. 24–25), ask students what they know about turtles and geese.

3. Ask them questions that connect their feelings with those of the characters in the story. For example, for the Skywoman story, it might be "Have you ever had the opportunity to help someone? How did it feel like when you did? What did you do?" Creating a physical image that appears in the story is also a good way to warm up. For example, for the Skywoman story, you might ask students to briefly work in pairs, where you can coach them to carry a heavy box in pantomime.

Development

1. Tell the story simply and dramatically in your own words. (See p. 13 for Storytelling Suggestions.) You can include additional characters if they fit into the story.

2. Have students pantomime some of the actions in slow motion—for example, the geese helping Skywoman as she is falling from the sky.

3. Flesh out the characters by guiding students to become "drama detectives." Ask them the *who, what, when, where,* and *why* questions. For example, Who is Turtle? What does he or she look like? Where does he or she live? Try out a little scene. For example, be Aunt Turtle or Uncle Turtle and, in role, ask the turtles in the story what they will do when Skywoman approaches them and how they feel about that. Talk and move in place like the Turtle, so the students get a hint of the character.

4. Tell the story again, this time with players standing or sitting in a circle. While the story is told, the young people become the objects and actions as they occur. For example, if you say, "The wind blew and blew and uprooted a tree," the students might become a tree and the voices of the wind.

5. Encourage students, at the appropriate times in the story, to "try on" the character while making up their own dialogue. For example, you can coach, "Partner up, please. One of you is Skywoman, and one of you is Turtle. Carry on a dialogue. What is happening? What does each character want? Who or what is blocking this desire or need?" Another example: "One of you is an object (such as a tree) or animal being made from clay. Work together. Say what you think the character would do and say." (Again, coach by asking questions about what is happening in the scene/moment, such as, What does the character want? What is each character feeling and how can these feelings be expressed in action? Where is the scene/moment taking place?)

Wrap-Up

Discuss with students how they felt acting out the story.

- What did they like best about acting out the story?

- Are there any parts they would like to do over? Why or why not? *Please note:* For students in Grades 3 to 6, you might want to use the drama rubric on p. 13 or devise your own.

- Ask some questions to assess students' understanding of the characters, feelings, and actions in the story. Sample questions: How does Skywoman get help to create the world? How do the geese help? How does Turtle help? How do the other animals, birds, and sea creatures help? What does this story show you about working together?

Extensions and Enrichments

- Art projects, such as drawing a scene from the story

- Vocabulary building

- Drama extensions, such as acting out scenes before or after the main action of the story

How to Transform Stories Into Plays With Students (Grades 3–6)

Because students of these ages are more comfortable with their writing, your goal for them can include script writing in addition to verbally dramatizing the stories.

Warm-Up

1. Relate the theme of the story to the lives of the students. Ask them questions that connect their feelings with feelings of the central character in the story. For example, in "The Three Questions" (pp. 48–50), you might ask one of the questions in

the story itself: What is the most important thing that the ruler of a country might accomplish? When is the best time to get something done? When working with many people, who is the most important one?

2. Motivate students in other ways. For example, you might connect the story with their interests or knowledge. In "The Three Questions," you could ask students what they know about Russia, tsars, hermits, or other tie-ins.

3. Provide a brief physical warm-up activity that relates to the story in some way and is age appropriate; for example, the Hermit in "The Three Questions" is thatching—in pantomime—the roof of his hut.

Development

1. Tell the story simply and dramatically in your own words (see p. 13 for Storytelling Suggestions). You can include additional characters if they fit into the story. For example, you might create a new character, such as the Prince's sister, who, fearing danger, tries to dissuade her brother from going to see the Hermit.

2. Provide improvisational opportunities for the students to try out in pairs. These paired character improvisations can include short scenes that take place before, during, or after the story. Doing these short improvisations gives the students a feel for the characters.

3. As an option, guide students to write the scenes that they have improvised. Provide the opportunity for the partners to share their written dialogues with each other or with the class as a whole.

4. Help students flesh out the characters by asking them the *who, what, when, where,* and *why* questions for the scenes that they create: Who is in the scene? How do the characters talk and move? What do they want? What prevents them from getting what they want?

5. Guide students to go on to another scene in the story, creating another key moment. For example, in "The Three Questions," why and how does the Prince disguise himself before visiting the Hermit? Review the *who, what, where, when, why* questions—for example, What is happening? What does each character want? Who or what gets in their way? Incorporate appropriate contributions made by the students.

6. Help students develop a series of scenes that can be acted out in sequence. Usually, scenes develop with the first one establishing a conflict, subsequent scenes developing the conflict; and the final scene providing a resolution to the conflict. Here are some sample options:

   • Divide the class into groups, each acting out a different version of the play.
   • Divide the class into groups, each acting out a different scene in the play.
   • Tell the story again and have the class simultaneously act out the various versions of the story, with all of its characters interacting with each other.

Wrap-Up

1. Guide students to reflect on the play and the process of making it come alive. Discuss with them how they felt acting out the story.

   • What did they like best about acting out the story?
   • Are there any parts that they would redo? Why?

2. Ask questions to access students' understanding of the characters, their feelings, and actions of the story, for example, how does the soldier in the woods contribute to the action of the story? You might ask in role (see pp. 2–3), as a visitor from another kingdom, what the students (in role as villagers) think of the Tsar, Prince, and Hermit before and after the Prince's visit to the Hermit.

3. Ask questions for students to reflect on thematic concepts of the story. For example,

- How does the Prince discover the real meaning of the three questions?
- What does the story show about the importance of positive leadership? About forgiveness?

Extensions and Enrichments

- Art projects, such as drawing a scene from the story

- Vocabulary building through eliciting new words from the story

- Drama extensions, such as acting out scenes before or after the main action of the story, writing out the improvised script or parts of it

Rubric for Revising: ACTED IT

Action: Clear to follow? Too little, too much? Does the play follow a sequence?

Characters: Were they believable, even if they were fantasy characters? Were their feelings expressed? How so?

Timing: Did the play's action go too fast or drag? Did actors listen to each other? Give some examples.

Environment: Did you establish clearly where the action takes place? How so?

Dialogue: Was the dialogue clear and believable, and did it fit the characters? Give some examples.

Imagination: Was the story acted out with imagination? Was it clear, interesting, and worthwhile to act out? Why or why not? Give some examples.

Teamwork: Did everyone work together to make the play work? How so?

Remember: When you work together, you win together!

Storytelling Suggestions

Find a special spot in the classroom where you can tell the story. Invite students to give the spot a special name, such as Story Corner, Story Circle, Global Magic, Peace Story Tree, and so on.

1. Tell the story dramatically, with vigor and zest. Catch the main elements, moments, and emotions of the story—be they suspenseful, humorful, beautiful—with your total being, including inflections and intensity, eye contact, and gestures.

2. Have a clear idea of the story's structure and the sequence of scenes. Tell the story directly. Make the characters come alive by using first-person dialogue whenever possible. Be as dramatic as the story demands. Always be sincere.

3. Do not memorize the story, except for certain key phrases or words, rhymes, chants, or jingles that are beloved and expected. When you tell your story, see it as pictures, one flowing into the next. Show the variation of characters through appropriately varied vocal inflections and gestures. In your telling of the tale, make references to the story's basic structure: beginning, middle, and end.

Variations

You may wish to use a flannel board when telling your story, especially with younger grades. It can be simply made from a Celotex building board and pieces of brightly colored cotton flannel or felt. A flannel board is an excellent device for children who are learning sequencing. Make sure to arrange your cutout characters, props, and scenic elements well in advance of the presentation.

Become Animals, Birds, and Sea Creatures

Goal: Given that quite a few stories in this section include animals, birds, and sea creatures, it is a good idea to take some time to help students create them with style and coordination.

Materials: Pictures of animals, birds, and sea creatures to stimulate students' imaginations.

1. Explain and model how students can create the essence of animals and birds through standing and stretching, squatting and hopping, and moving and miming in small groups.

2. Guide students to explore the following formations as warm-ups or in connection with a specific story.

Standing and Stretching

Cranes: Guide students to put their right feet forward, extend their right arms, and curl their fingers. Eyes should be on the curled-up fingers. Then have them do it in reverse: put their left feet forward, extend their left arms, curl their fingers, and focus on the fingers and stand proud as a crane or heron. Coach, "Make soft humming sounds."

Small birds: Coach, "Stand in place. Imagine you are perched on a tree. Slowly stretch out one of your arm wings; then stretch out the other one. Flap your wings very slowly and then increase the fluttering. Take a step. You're flying in the air. Stay in place. Alternate the intensity of the flapping. Let's hear some chirping or other sounds your birds might make."

Hawks: Coach, "Move your wings freely, but s-l-o-w-l-y. Practice moving your arm wings together and take a few circular steps in slow motion as you fix your eyes intently on some object in the room. Turn your space into a specific kind of natural environment, for example, a forest with other hawks or birds circling around."

Standing, Stepping, and Sliding

Horses: Coach, "Stand in place. Pantomime holding and pulling the reins in your hands. Step forward s-l-o-w-l-y as your horse rears its head and trots, prances, or gallops." Help students, as they stand in place, to give the illusion of the moving horse with rider atop. Coach, "Slide your left foot forward, followed by sliding your right foot forward. Then slide your right foot forward, fol-

14

lowed by sliding your left foot to the right foot as the horse prances, gallops, or trots. Keep on alternating your sliding feet and add some neighing sounds." For students to be a horse without a rider, coach, "Place one foot behind the other, bend the forward knee, bend your body forward, tilt your head to the side, saying *neigh*."

Bears: Coach, "Stand tall. Bend over slightly. Keep your bear arms close to your body. Move—or should we say *lumber*—around a bit. Sometimes you might feel like placing your hands on the floor or moving around on all fours. Make some bear-grunting sounds."

Monkeys: Coach, "Stand straight, bend over slightly, let your monkey arms hang limp at your sides at first, then in various swinging motions. Make some soft monkey sounds to go along with the movements."

Standing and Squatting

Ducks: Coach, "Squat fully to the floor. Hold on to both of your ankles with your hands. Take small steps and waddle from side to side, to and fro. Add some *quacks* as you do."

Frogs: Coach, "Squat with hands touching the floor. Hop around and add a *ribbit, ribbit* sound as you do."

Kangaroos: Coach, "Squat down halfway to the floor. Place your hands on your knees. Hop forward and hop again."

Rabbits: Coach, "Squat down, halfway to the floor. Extend both of your arms out in one sweeping motion. Hop with both feet."

Elephants: Coach, "Walk on all fours. Once in a while, use one of your arms as the elephant's trunk."

In Pairs or in Small Groups

Students should wear comfortable gym attire for the following exercises.

Caterpillars: Players work in pairs. Partners place their hands on the floor. The trick is to get those eight legs working together without partners touching each other.

Spiders: Coach, "Team up with two or three students, extend your arms and hands forward, link them with your teammates. Very loosely and smoothly, wave them *s-l-o-w-l-y* around as you make harmonious spidery sounds."

Whales: Works well in groups of ten to fifteen. Coach, "Stand in front of each other in a vertical line. The student at the head of the line becomes the whale's head; the last student, the whale's fluke. All players bend over slightly. Do not touch each other but move together forward in *s-l-o-w* harmonious steps. Make a soft sound together."

Variations

Encourage students on their own to create other animals, birds, and creatures of the sea. In small groups, they will enjoy transforming into environments for the animals, birds, and sea creatures, such as a forest for the animals and birds or a pond for sea creatures. Invite students to show their environments one at a time.

Extensions and Enrichments

- Invite students to create, with paper and chalk, environments for their animals, birds, and sea creatures. For example, using butcher paper, they might draw a colorful collage or mural that suggests the environment of what they have made with their bodies and sounds.

More Helpful Tips: Becoming Animals, Birds, and Sea Creatures

- Encourage students to follow their own creative impulses when becoming the various creatures, to go along with their own interpretations, to freely explore the images they come up with— and, above all, to enjoy the experience.

- Help them to consider, during revision, the specific circumstances related to the creatures they are portraying. For example, what is the creature doing in the moment—sleeping, working, playing? When is it doing it and why?

- Guide students to show what they have in mind through varying their
Body shapes
Size
Movement and sounds

  For example, is a tree frog just sitting, a bull frog wading in the water, a toad hopping around on land? Is a horse a bucking bronco, a free-roaming mustang, a circus pony? Is a tiny bee speeding to a flower, a large elephant moving slowly through the jungle, a lioness feeding her little cubs by a river bank? How does the particular creature use the space around it, and what spatial pathways do they take to fulfill their objectives? Make sure the speed and force that the students apply to their movements and sounds have a natural flow.

- Ask questions to help students discover new things and apply what they know in their creative efforts. For example, coach, "What do the feet of a duck look like, and how can you show that with your hands? What do the feet of caterpillars look like? Working together, how can you show these ideas through the shape of your bodies and movement?"

  Guide students to further realize their visions. For example, coach, "See how far you can move your elbows away from each other to become the wings of a hawk. What is the hawk looking for? How does it fly? What body levels and spatial directions can you use to show how the hawk can fly and reach its destination? Why is it going there?"

  Guide younger students to "grow" imaginatively into their animals, limb by limb from a squatting position, emerging like flowers in the sunshine.

- Help students access and appreciate their own efforts by having them ask questions such as the following: "Have I stretched my body and mind to come up with the most interesting and varied gestures, sounds, and movements?"

Using Pantomime

- Conduct a discussion on the nature of pantomime. Make sure students know that pantomime is communication through body language—gestures, movement, and facial expression.

- Form a circle so that students can see each other clearly, and have them talk with their bodies. Use such examples as
How do you say with your fingers, "This potato is hot!"
How do you say with your feet, "I'm waiting"?
How do you say, "This flower smells sweet"?

- Encourage students to practice *activity mime*, working with objects, and *fantasy mime*, becoming objects.

- Guide students to make sure that their imaginary objects are as real as possible when handling them. They should make pictures of the objects in their minds and pay attention to the objects' surfaces (shapes, sizes, and textures) and weights. They should especially be aware of leaving space between their fingers when holding up their imaginary objects and of following through and not dropping them.

- Guide them to practice the activity mime first with actual objects, whenever possible and if available. Students will be better able to create illusions of space by actually handling the objects, such as by picking up and passing around a ball or glass.

- Guide students to practice the fantasy mime, individually or in pairs, by transforming into a ball, glass, or any other object. Students have already done so in story enactments; now they make sure to show the appropriate emotions, such as being a tired or spirited ball.

Creating a Tableau

Goal: Students will be able to work together in groups of three to four to cooperatively create frozen life scenes and silent story scenes.
Materials: Human bodies become the clay for story scenes.

Warm-Up

- Ask students, standing in place, to imagine that they are standing in front of an apple tree. Have them show the frozen moment as they pick apples from the tree.

- Ask older students, in groups, to re-create and reflect on the moment when they decided to pick the apples. Discuss motivations for picking the apples from the tree. Are they hungry? Are they workers picking the fruit to package and sell? Are they picking the apples to feed those who have no food? Are the apples turning brown and overripe and so need to be picked and sorted? Are they visiting an orchard to pick apples for fun?

- Ask, Who are the characters in the tableau? What is their relationship? How is each of the aforementioned motivations manifested through the body language of the participants? Is the weather hot? Is it cold? Is it raining?

Development

1. Ask for three volunteers to demonstrate a frozen moment from the story you have told. For example, in "The Animals, Birds, and Sea Creatures Help Skywoman Create the World" (pp. 24–25), direct them to become two of the animals creating the shape of a mountain (the third student). Ask three different volunteers to create another frozen moment, suggested by the class. This time, guide the students as they shape the moment.

2. Explain to the class that they are the directors of the scene. With kindergarten and first-grade students, you can serve as the director, with some of the students assisting you. Guide students to work with the suggestions of the group regarding how the scene should look. Help them to closely observe the nonverbal details of the scene, such as the opened- or closed-hand position of a character, the expression on a character's face, the direction in which a head is turned. Coach students

19

to get feedback from the group regarding how the meaning in the scene changes when subtle variations are made.

3. Guide students to work in groups of four. Player A acts as the director of the scene. Assign a different scene from the story to each group. Give students about 5 minutes to work on the scene.

Wrap-Up

1. Ask the groups to show select scenes as you retell the story.

2. Discuss with the students each of the scenes, allowing them to add dialogue to the characters whom they are portraying.

Extensions and Enrichments

1. Create a "sculpture museum" in which players from half the class can walk around and enjoy the tableau of topics, such as outer space, the Middle Ages, current events, and so on. Encourage students to express what they liked about their classmates' creations.

2. Invite them to write a title and a short paragraph explaining the group's tableau.

3. As their groups become more comfortable with this activity, increase the number of students in the group to four or five and allow them to work collaboratively as the directors of their scenes. Guide students to further explore their frozen moments by giving their poses titles, asking the observing students to express what the tableau characters are thinking, and playing a scene forward from the frozen tableau moment.

Making Classroom Scenery, Costumes, and Simple Props

The poems and stories in this book are designed, for the most part, to be enacted with dialogue and pantomime and without the use of real objects or scenery. However, there may be a time when you want the class to take the dramatization further by adding simple costumes, props, and scenery. Here are some suggestions.

Classroom Scenery and Simple Props

Classroom scenery and simple props should be inexpensive and imaginative. For example, a few set pieces of trees might represent a whole forest, or a ruler can become a spoon, flag, pen, or baton. In the words of Ralph Waldo Emerson, "Art teaches to convey a larger sense by simpler symbols." In this respect, even a single stylized tree could suggest a forest. Scrounging around for inexpensive scenery is one of the chief delights of theater on any level. For example, a chair wrapped in aluminum foil makes an authentic royal throne for the Tsar in the story. Put a few chairs together covered with painted cardboard, and you have an instant Hermit's hut. The chalkboard, with the aid of colored chalk, can become the background for all kinds of settings. A "Scrounging Begins at Home" contest is fun. Magic markers, cloth of dazzling colors, cotton balls, oaktag, scissors, paste, and so on can prove quite useful in your overall design. Lay out the organized materials, and let the kids go to town.

If you plan to extend your informal class session to a more ambitious production for invited guests, here are some additional ideas. Manufacturers or store owners often have odds and ends left over that they can donate to your production, such rolls of fabric or paper, yarn, sheets of corrugated cardboard, bubble plastic, and empty cartons. Think imaginatively about your materials. For example, an old beach chair made out of vinyl webbing can be unwoven into strands. The resulting strings can be tied onto a overhead clothesline or grid to make a forest. Cartons can be undone and turned into wonderful 3-D or flattened shapes for painting. The cartons themselves can be stacked, glued together, or opened and interlocked.

Old sheets and table cloths can be cut into different-sized squares and rectangles, painted and hung by clothes pins from lines that are crisscrossed around the room. As you hang the pieces of fabrics, see what happens when they descend into freefall formations. Collaborative environments can be assembled from discarded objects, such sheets of flat or crumpled newspaper or even from old neck ties. Mismatched discarded chairs, painted in bright colors and rearranged into different vertical and horizontal formations, can represent almost anything, from seats in a school bus to a magical tree trunk, an old crooked house, a hut, or a cave.

Costume Ideas

Again, the key words are *imaginative* and *inexpensive*. With a simple stroke, try to convey the essence of the larger whole. In the classroom, you may wish to keep a costume box, from which you can adapt clothing at hand. For example, leftover tapestries, fancy draperies, table cloths, and discarded curtains can be reworked to serve the needs of the classroom play. Discarded clothing pieces of any vintage—such as shirts, jackets, skirts, hats, and belts that are still in good, clean condition—can spark the imagination and actually help students to create characters on the spot.

Crêpe paper, crinkled newspaper, oilcloth for leather trimmings, and burlap (which when redone in silver paint makes excellent plate armor) can be used for period costuming. Belts can be made from oaktag or felt. The crown for a king can be constructed from gilded oaktag or cardboard. Sandals for soldiers can be made by tying laces around the legs.

The simplest materials treated imaginatively can transform the ordinary into the beautiful, such as when cheesecloth is turned into lace and dried-out cotton flannel becomes velvet.

Keep in Mind . . .

S*et* your goals clearly so that students can accomplish them.

P*lan* your work carefully, using a framework of warm-up, development, and wrap-up.

A*rrange* your materials so that they are handy.

R*emember* to keep the focus on content within a dramatic framework so that there is a good flow of creative energy.

K*now* that, above all, drama deals with the expression and understanding of feelings.

SPARK the students' imaginations to create.

CHAPTER TWO
CARING AND SHARING

D rama is a collaborative effort, one in which every individual's contribution to creating a play is respected and valued. When people work closely together in a meaningful shared process, there is a high degree of caring. Players become sensitive to each other's feelings and to connecting interpretations of what a story says and what it communicates to each individual.

While working on this book, we often saw children's faces aglow after acting out the stories. During feedback, they expressed their feelings in different ways, but the joy of cooperation was a common response:

- "The story had conflict, but we worked it out together."

- "You had to listen to each other—or there couldn't be a play."

- "It was fun to always have someone on your side."

Sharing one's imagination with others is a vital part of the process of transforming a story into a play. Because stories and plays deal with language, listening carefully to each other's ideas is important in the early stages of creation. Later, it is exciting to improvise and listen to dialogue as it flows spontaneously, moment to moment, within the framework of the story's structure. It is equally exciting, and often beautiful, to share how the body, with gesture and movement, can become such an expressive instrument.

In these ways, young people share the process of becoming the very story they are enacting. When they can do that, with all the pride that goes along with it, the joyful afterglow is not soon forgotten. Neither is what they have learned and how they can apply the sharing and caring to other life experiences.

Story: "Animals, Birds, and Sea Creatures Help Skywoman Create the Earth"—Native American Myth (Grades K–3)

Skywoman and the creatures work together to form Earth, using lots of cooperation.

In the land above the sky, there was a strong wind that blew so hard that one day it uprooted a tree. A shadowy hole, difficult to see, was created. Skywoman, walking by the tree, fell through the hole and began to fall into the sky of the land below. She felt frightened, at first, that she might hurt herself. But as she fell, some geese that were flying by slowed her fall, and so she landed safely on a giant Turtle that came from the waters below. "Let us make the Earth," Skywoman said to Turtle. "I will use what mud we have, and then we can search for more."

"You can smear the mud on my back," Turtle said.

"Good idea," said Skywoman.

"When we run out," said Turtle, "we will find more at the bottom of the water."

The geese smeared mud on the back of Turtle. Then, together, they dived into the water for more mud. When the ducks saw this, they joined Turtle and Skywoman in getting mud from the bottom of the ocean floor. The ducks and geese put the mud in their beaks, brought up some mud, and spread it all over Turtle's shell. The ducks said to the geese, and the geese said to the ducks, "Let's go down and get some more mud to spread on the back of Turtle."

When this happened, Turtle said, as did Skywoman, "Thank you, ducks. Thank you, geese."

The ducks and geese replied, "You're welcome, Turtle. You're welcome, Skywoman."

The beavers, who were great builders, worked hard and long, too, to make the land above the shell bigger and bigger. The Earth we live on was beginning to take shape.

Turtle said, and so did Skywoman, "Thank you, too, beavers, for helping out."

The beavers replied, "You're welcome, Skywoman. You're welcome, Turtle."

Everybody was so busy now. Everybody was greatly excited. They felt good. This world that they were creating was growing and growing. Now other animals, birds, and sea creatures were busy building mountains, making lakes and valleys—until, finally, they had made the whole round Earth, while all the time Skywoman sat safely on the back of Turtle.

And it is said that to this very day Turtle still holds Earth up on its shell.

Act Out the Story

Goal: Students will work together to act out a Native American myth that focuses on cooperation and teamwork.

Materials: None.

Warm-Up: Form a Peaceful Globe

1. Ask the students, "Have you ever felt that you needed someone's help to do something? How did you feel? What did you do?"

2. Explain that they will be acting out a Native American myth in which Skywoman needs the help of animals, birds, and sea creatures to create the Earth.

3. Divide the class into the three groups. Ask each group to show, by means of movement, sounds, and mime, one physical aspect of the globe. For example, one group of students may make a circle, hold hands, move slowly, and emit soft sounds that express Earth. Another group of students may team up to become rivers by outstretching their connecting arms. A third group of students might create mountains by extending their

arms vertically with interlocking finger tips. The students may freeze the scene into a tableau (see pp. 18–20).

Development

1. Tell the story. In role, you may wish to play a tribal storyteller.

2. Help students to explore creating the different movements and sounds of the animals, birds, and sea creatures that appear in the story.

3. Guide students to flesh out the main characters. Ask questions about Skywoman and Turtle: *Who are they? What do they want? What does she look like? How does she move? What does she want? Why?* Students portraying Skywoman should sit at the side of Turtle. Challenge students to add on to the Turtle without touching so that Turtle transforms into small circles of players becoming features of the land and so that it eventually evolves into one large circle with players holding hands to depict the

Creating the environment for a peaceful globe, mountains, and rivers in the Native American creation story "Animals, Birds, and Sea Creatures Help Skywoman Create the Earth." (Photo: Mark Solkoff)

Earth. Turtle can also be made by students sitting in a circle and holding hands. They can smear mud in pantomime on the part of the shell in front of them.

4. Tell the story again, incorporating ideas from the students.

Focus on Content

- Focus on the part in the story when the animals pitched in to create the world.

- Ask, "How are the animals and other creatures able to accomplish their task? How was working together the key for the animals to accomplish their task?"

- Ask, "How are students creating the play like the animals and birds working together to create the world with Skywoman?"

- Ask why cooperation is so important when working on a shared goal. Encourage students to give examples.

Wrap-Up

1. Guide students to reflect on the experience of acting out the story. Was it interesting? Was the play clear? Did they show imagination in acting out the story? Are there any parts that they would like to see done differently? Why?

2. Have them, as an option, act out the water or animals in pairs during appropriate times as the story is told again.

Extensions and Enrichments

- Invite students to draw their impressions of the story, incorporating their feelings about it.

- Encourage them to make up a chant or song that can be integrated with the telling of the story (see the following section, More Helpful Tips: Sounds in Harmony).

- Challenge older students (Grades 3–6) to add a "word chant" (see p. 29).

More Helpful Tips: Sounds in Harmony

This exercise helps students of all ages to work together in harmony and to experiment with making sounds that might be used with chanting in the Skywoman story.

Goal: Students will work together to make a human band of harmonious sounds.

Materials: Pictures of musical instruments optional.

1. *Explain or model:* Start by having each student in the class choose an instrument to play and practice holding and playing it in pantomime without making a sound.

2. Guide students to softly verbalize the sounds that the instruments would make.

3. Direct the students with the same instruments to stand or sit together and to practice making harmonious soft sounds while playing their mimed instruments.

4. Form a class human band by having different students act as conductors who point to the different instrument sections or to solo instrumentalists to play on cue. Guide students to take turns as conductors, holding fingers to their lips to indicate a softer sound or moving their hands and arms to make louder, shorter, or stretched-out sounds.

Extensions and Enrichments

- Encourage students to play a variety of songs, short commercial jingles, and even original songs.

- Guide students to make some audio recordings of some of the songs that the band plays.

Make a Word Chant . . .

Divide the class into three groups. Guide each group to choose an appropriate word or phrase to repeat. Coach each group to vocalize the word or phrase on a different sound level—that is, low, medium, or high. Choose one student to act as the conductor, and create a traditional round, with each group beginning its section in the middle of the last group's section. The combinations of the levels of sound and the words or phrases can accompany the story enactment or a movement or pantomime piece. Coach the groups to add staccato sounds and smooth sounds, as well as loud, soft, high, low clicks, hums, and clucks—whatever fits the particular mood and characterization.

. . . And Make a Homemade Rhythm Band

To help bring alive the chanting in the story, use instruments already in the classroom. These include sleigh bells, wood blocks, drums, triangles, cymbals, jingle clogs, rhythm slides, tambourines, rhythm bells, tone blocks, and clappers. One's hands are probably the most creative rhythm instruments for clapping and snapping.

Children love making their own instruments. For example, coffee cans filled with pinto beans, stones, rice, or alfalfa seeds make excellent rattlers, as do dried gourds with their seeds still intact. Homemade drums can be easily made by covering oatmeal boxes with construction paper. Drum beaters? A stick of dowel covered with rubber bands and yarn. A terrific tambourine can be created by gluing together two paper plates filled with dried beans and inserting Popsicle sticks for handles.

When the instruments have been selected, have the students form a small instrumental group to accompany the telling and enactment of the story. The band sits in a semicircle, following the action of the story.

Left—bells and triangles
Center—sticks and blocks
Right—tambourines, cymbals, drums
Left–beyond bells-castanets between cymbals and tambourines

- Encourage students to experiment with combinations of human bands, word chants, and homemade bands.

29

Story: "The Friendly Forest" (Grades K–2)

Once upon a time, through the early morning mist, the sun rose high in the sky. *(One student in the center of the circle rises slowly, forming a sun with arms and hands.)* Its golden rays warmed the Friendly Forest.

Look up to the sky—birds of all kinds, of all colors, big and small, are flying to the Friendly Forest. *(Students fly in toward the circle.)* Hear their sound: "We are the birds, we fly all around. To the Friendly Forest / Hear our sound."

The birds landed on their favorite trees and bushes. *(Students, using varied body shapes and spatial levels, transform into different-sized trees, bushes, and shrubs.)* There were elms, oaks, weeping willows, and all kinds of bushes and flowers.

Near the trees was a beautiful range of snow-capped mountains. *(Students gently touch the raised fingertips of the students next to them to form triangular mountain peaks.)* You could feel the frosty cold air of the mountains. Running below the mountains was a river *(Sitting in the circle, students gently lower and join their hands in the circle)*, so quiet you could hear the sounds of all kinds of fishes in the river. *(Students use their hands and arms to make the shapes of different-sized fishes.)* There were bass, perch, and trout and other kinds of fish.

At one end of the river there was a small but sturdy bridge. *(Two students stretch out their arms and gently interlock hands.)* On the other side of the river *(Students gently join hands again)*, there was a lighthouse *(Several students join hands and form the circular base of the lighthouse while one student stands in the middle and slowly moves his or her head like a light beam)*. It shed its light at night on the beautiful flowers in the Friendly Forest. *(Students become all kinds of flowers with varied body shapes and spatial levels as the light shines on them.)*

People also enjoyed coming to the Friendly Forest. They respected the natural wonders there, and they also respected each other. *(Students, in pairs, play the mirror exercise; see p. 39.)*

There were different types of animals in the Friendly Forest. There was a Mountain Lion. *(Student playing Mountain Lion comes out to center of the circle.)* "I am a Mountain Lion / I sit on my throne." *(Student crouches.)* "I'm king of the forest / But I am not alone!" *(Student goes back to perimeter of circle and sits.)*

There were two cute dancing Bear Cubs. *(Two students come out as cubs.)* "I am the brother / I am the sister / Bears / We also live here." *(They do a little playful cub dance and then return to the perimeter of the circle, where they sit.)*

There was also a Red Fox. *(Student comes out to the center of the circle as Red Fox.)* "I am a Red Fox / I live by the rocks!" *(Student returns to the perimeter of the circle.)*

On the other side of the river there was a town. The town was having a circus, which had a big Elephant. At night, the Elephant would lumber from the town to join the other animals in the Friendly Forest. *(Student becomes Elephant and lumbers into the center of the circle.)* "I am an Elephant / I also care!"

You saw that big Elephant. But there were also little creatures in the Friendly Forest—like Busy the Bee. *(Student runs quickly around the inner circle but slowly enough for the words to be heard clearly.)* "I'm Busy the Bee, I'm Busy the Bee / I'm so fast you can't catch me!") *(Student returns to the perimeter of circle and sits.)*

There were also some Bunnies in the Friendly Forest. *(Four or five students go to the center of the circle as Bunnies.)* You can hear their sound: "We are the bunnies / We hop all around / We're so soft / You can hardly hear our sound." *(They hop back to their places in the circle.)*

There were also some Frogs in the Friendly Forest. *(Four or five students leap carefully over to the mimed lily ponds.)* You can hear their sounds: "We are Frogs. There are four of us / We sit in the pond / And make a lot of fuss!" *(They leap back to their places in the circle and sit.)*

Remember how I told you that people came to the Friendly Forest? Well, one day a brother and a sister, after a full day of camping, packed up all their things. *(Two students pantomime packing up their things in backpacks.)* They remembered that they had to completely put out their camp fire. They poured water over the camp fire to make sure all the flames were out. *(They pantomime pouring water from water cans.)* They even stamped the ground to make sure that the fire was completely out. The brother said, "I think the fire is all out, Sister." And she said, "Good job, Brother. Let's go home." So they left for home. *(Students return to their places in the circle.)*

But shortly after they left, a great wind started up. *(Students make the sound of the wind.)* A little, little spark of a flame flickered. *(With their fingers, students make the little shape of the spark, accompanied by appropriate sounds.)* The flames grew larger and larger. *(With motions and soft sounds, students enlarge flames.)* It was not the two campers' fault that the spark caught fire. A big wind started to blow the flames so that they got bigger and bigger. One flame led to another, and they were hard to stop. *(Students slowly move their fingers and arms in stylized motion.)*

Busy the Bee saw the flames and flew over to one of the Frogs and shouted, "There's a fire, there's a fire!"

The Frog shouted to one of the Bunnies, "Oh dear, oh my, there's fire!"

The Bunny shouted over to the Brother Bear, "Oh my, oh dear, there's a fire!" and the Brother Bear Cub shouted over to his sister, "There's a fire, there's a fire!"

The Sister Bear Cub shouted over to the Red Fox, "Hurry, hurry, there's fire!" The Red Fox shouted to the Mountain Lion, "There's a fire, there's a fire!"

The Mountain Lion climbed quickly to the top of the mountain and in his biggest voice ever shouted all the way to the town to the elephant, "Help, help! There's a fire in the Friendly Forest! Help! Help!"

The Elephant went as fast he could to the Friendly Forest. He quickly went to the pond *(Students join hands and become the pond)* and sucked water into his trunk *(Students make the sound).* Then the Elephant went around to all the flames and put the flames out and—slowly, miracle of miracles—the trees, bushes, and flowers began to grow again and stand proudly in the Friendly Forest. But it was not a miracle, because all the animals had worked together to put the fire out. And once more the sun shone brilliantly on the trees, flowers, and bushes and on all the animals, big and small. And that, my friends, is the story of the Friendly Forest.

Act Out the Story

Recommendation: Spread this story over two or three sessions.

Goal: Students will act out a story using transformational story about animals banding together to put out a forest fire.

Materials: None.

Warm-Up

1. Ask students for examples of how they have helped each other in times of need.

2. Explain that they will act out a story showing how animals in a forest helped each other in a time of great need.

3. Ask some students to demonstrate how they would form a river by linking their hands gently. Practice with them, doing it gently.

Development

1. Tell the story.

2. Assign different students the parts of the Mountain Lion, two Bear Cubs, the Red Fox, Busy the Bee, the Elephant, the Bunnies, the Frogs, the Lighthouse, and the Bridge. Everyone plays the roles of Birds, Trees and Shrubbery, Flowers, Mountains, the River, and the Pond.

3. Guide the students to "try on" the different animals and environments. Retell different parts of the stories and ask the students to experiment on the spot with the movements and sounds associated with the animals.

4. As you tell the complete story, follow the stage directions and guide the students to act out what is happening in the story. Redo certain parts if they are not clear.

5. Tell the story several times with different combinations of students taking the parts.

6. Ask questions like these: "Are you stretching your bodies and voices to become all the characters as best you can? Are you using your imaginations to the fullest?"

Kindergartners make a bridge in "The Friendly Forest." (Photo: Carmine Tabone)

Wrap-Up

Focus on Content

1. Ask the students what they learned from listening to the story and acting it out.

2. Ask if there are any parts of the story that they would like to redo. Why?

3. Encourage students to include their variations if they choose to redo parts.

Extensions and Enrichments

1. Suggest to students that they draw pictures about the Friendly Forest.

2. Encourage them to add other animals and creatures to the story when they make their drawings.

More Helpful Tips: How to Use Transformations

At the heart of the creative drama process on any age level, players go through a variety of changes. Students change into actors, who change into characters, who undergo a variety of actions and feelings. Additionally, in the early grades, while acting out stories, students most likely will play more than one character as well as a variety of environments in which the characters interact. For example, in the Friendly Forest, one second a student is flying as a bird, a few seconds later he or she is a tree, and seconds later a flowing river.

In creative drama we call these varied creative changes *transformations*. In making these transformations, it is important that students feel pride in creating beautiful pictures that are full of life. This happens when they use different body shapes and motions that are fluid and clear. For example, in the Friendly Forest, a student may first become a tree of her or his own creation. Then, teaming up with a partner, the student moves her or his arms and hands to slowly link up with the student on either side, gently touching fingertips to form pointed snow-capped mountains.

To help you work with students to make clear and smooth transitions, we suggest that you

- Model, using your body movements, demonstrating how transformations work.

- Experiment with students as to how they can devise their own transformational images.

- Guide students to polish their transformational images so that incorporated into their creations are appropriate body shapes, spatial levels, and flows of energy with just the right speed and flow of energy.

"Why Do the Young Hawks Cry?"—Native American Poem (All Grades)

The following is a poem for all ages that movingly shows why it is important to feel protected.

> Why do the young hawks cry,
> As someone in the sky flies to them?
> From our hearts we offer thanks
> As the mother hawk flies to her young
> Who cry for joy as she slowly descends
> And rests with her nestlings

Act Out the Poem

Goal: Students will act out a limited-action poem about caring.
Materials: Copies of the poem and pictures of hawks.

Warm-Up

1. Ask students if they have ever felt the need to feel safe. How did they feel? What did they do?
(You can also ask them to mirror each other's movements—see p. 39.)

2. Discuss with the class who could be in the nest and why it is important that the nest be protected.

3. Ask students to imagine that they are hawks flapping their wings, protecting their young. Ask, "Why is it important for the mother hawks to protect their young?"

Development

1. Direct students to sit in a circle. Read the poem aloud.

Focus on Content

2. Guide students to flesh out the main characters. Ask, "Why are the young hawks crying? What do they want? When the mother eagle hears the crying, how does she feel, and what does she do? Why?"

Student flying as a hawk in the poem "Why Do the Young Hawks Cry?"
(Photo: Mark Solkoff)

3. Divide the class into subgroups, each one with a mother hawk and a number of young hawks. Guide the young hawks to cry softly when the first line is read as the young hawks flap their wings slowly. Coach the mother hawks to hover in the air (standing in place, flapping wing arms in slow motion) to create a beautiful tableau (see pp. 18–20). For older students, guide each group of young hawks (with their mother hawk) to create a tableau that shows the moment that the hawks notice that their mother is coming toward them. Working with each group individually while the others observe as audience, ask the students to move into a pose (to the count of five backward) and hold the pose in a frozen moment, as if a camera were snapping their photograph. Ask, "What title would you give this tableau? If the

hawks could talk, what would each say to the mother hawk?" (you might tap each hawk on the shoulder-wing for a response). Ask, "What do you think the mother hawk would say to her young?"

4. Guide students to enact the rest of the poem with appropriate movement and sounds. Repeat the sound movement poem.

Wrap-Up

After the poem has been enacted, ask the class again why it is important for the young hawks to be protected and why it is important for the mother hawks to do so.

Extensions and Enrichments

- Have students recite the poem or parts of it in choral unison. When you coach your students to do so, make sure they speak together slowly and clearly and with feeling.

- Suggest that students capture the essence of the poem through drawings or clay work.

Poem: "Me, Myself, and I" (Grades K–6)

When is it good to be alone, and when is it good to be with others?

> Sometimes it's great
> To be all alone—
> Without even my telephone
> Other times though
> It's hard to rely
> On just me, myself, and I
> (Can you tell me why?)

Act Out the Poem

Goal: Students will explore together, through sound and movement, how it feels to be alone, as well as the importance of being with others.

Materials: Copies of the poem.

Warm-Up: Mirror, Mirror

1. Direct students to stand and face each other in pairs. One is designated Player A, the other Player B.

2. Guide players, facing their partners in pairs, to silently describe to themselves the color of their partner's eyes and any other distinguishing facial features, such as dimples, eyelashes, frowns, smiles, and so on.

3. Ask Player A to start the slow movement of the head. Player B is to mime Player A's movements as much as possible. Coach, "Go *s-l-o-w-l-y*. One starts; the other partner copies; then switch, with the other starting. Do not discuss with each other what you are doing. No talking at all. Trust each other to take turns, starting and following the movements in one smooth, flowing action." Ask students how it felt to follow their partners' motions.

Mirror, Mirror: Warm-up for enacting the poem "Me, Myself, and I." (Photo: Milton Polsky)

Development

Focus on Content

1. Discuss with class which of their experiences or the experiences of others might make them say, "Sometimes it's great to be alone." Ask if they know someone who at some time did not feel that they needed other people.

---

2. Divide the class into three groups: one to recite the first two lines, one to recite the second line, and one to recite the next three lines. Everyone will then recite the last line, "Can you tell me why?"

3. Guide students to stand in three horizontal lines when the lines are recited, except during the last line. When the line "Can you tell me why?" is recited, the three subgroups join hands and make a circle—and s-l-o-w-l-y mirror each other.

Wrap-Up

1. Discuss the experience with the class: "What is the main idea of the poem, and how did the enactment of the poem reinforce the main idea?"

2. Repeat the enactment with different students composing the subgroups.

Extensions and Enrichments

- Encourage students to make up their own poems about being alone and with other people.

- Guide them to make an artistic mural expressing their feelings about the poem or one of their own.

Poem: "Helpful/Unhelpful Advice" by Howard Berland (Grades 3–6)

Is it always good to try to be helpful?

Have you ever once tried
To be someone's bright guide
Where there's a need for a kind helping hand?
Well, I tried it this spring
Yes, to do a good thing—
To help my friend at her lemonade stand.
Oh, dear, no one would buy
And she didn't know why—
Aw, my poor friend was ready to cry!
I said, "Take my advice,
You don't have enough ice
And that's why nobody will buy!"
So I emptied my freezer
I was sure that would please her,
A full bucket of ice I made
But she said, "I don't need it
Because I succeeded,
Sold, all my uncold lemonade!"
Wow! So how did she do it?
I sure wish I knew it . . .
She laughed! "No secret that is so deep—
Without enough ice
I just lowered the price—
They all wanted a drink that was cheap!"
Well, it doesn't take long
To ask if I was wrong
To bring her all that ice.
I wonder, too, how her customers felt—
Did their warm lemonade taste so nice?

Act Out the Poem

Goal: Students act out, using pantomime, a poem with a surprising twist about when it is—and when it is not—appropriate to help people.

Materials: None.

Warm-Up With Pantomime

1. Ask students how they think lemonade is made. Ask: "What ingredients are needed to make it?"

2. Guide them to pantomime making lemonade—for example, squeezing already-cut lemons into a pitcher of water.

3. Ask students to share, in pantomime, how they would pour the lemonade that they have made. Play the game "Start the action and turn it into something else that helps with the first action," such as "Sip soup with a spoon." Ask the student next in the circle to take that action and turn it into something different that helps complete the first action, such as washing the soup bowl. Call on other students to start and complete a simple action.

Development

1. Ask students to give some examples of their trying to help someone and if their help was successful or not.

2. Divide the class into four groups: the student playing the friend who has the lemonade stand; students playing the friend of the character who has the lemonade stand; students playing lemonade-stand customers; and the group that recites the poem while it is acted out in pantomime by the other three groups.

3. Direct each group to create and practice the pantomime of each of its characters.

4. Guide the groups to recite the poem slowly as each group member acts out his or her pantomime.

Focus on Content

5. Ask students how they feel about the question that the friend asks in the last stanza. In role, they can answer as customers, discussing why they bought warm lemonade at a reduced price. Ask students to explain what they mean by helping people in time of need and to give some examples. Encourage diversity of responses.

Wrap-Up

Guide students to act out the poem again but this time with different students playing the characters of the lemonade-stand owner, the friend, and the customers.

Extensions and Enrichments

- Encourage the students to write and enact their own poems about helping—and not helping.

Mandala Picture Project (Grades 3–6)

How can art help us to work together?

Goal: Students will become aware of the importance of cooperation, through art, improvisation, and script writing.

Materials: Square pieces of paper (approximately four inches by four inches), Magic Markers, large piece of craft paper (approximately four feet by four feet), glue, paint, markers.

Warm-Up

1. Ask the students, "What do you think the word *cooperation* means? Give some examples."

2. Explain that this week they will be working on creating a class mandala and a story (e.g., "Skywoman," pp. 24–25; or "The

Quails' Story," pp. 63–65). Both illustrate the importance of people working together to get something done. The first activity is to create a mandala.

Development

1. Show the class some examples of mandalas from around the world, found on the Internet. Explain that there are mandalas that we see in our everyday lives, such as manhole covers, stained glass windows, and each other's eyes.

2. Divide the class into pairs. Pass out one square of paper (four inches by four inches) to each pair and give out the markers. Ask the students to become either an A or a B.

   - Demonstrate how to fold the square of paper in half so that it becomes a triangle. Student A does this fold and passes

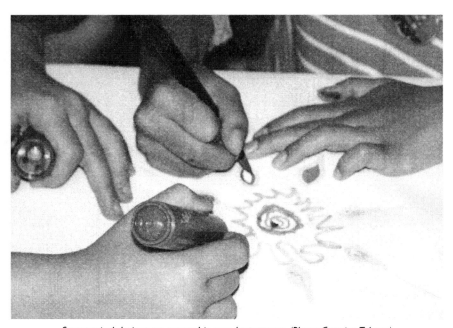

Symmetrical designs are created in turn by partners. (Photo: Carmine Tabone)

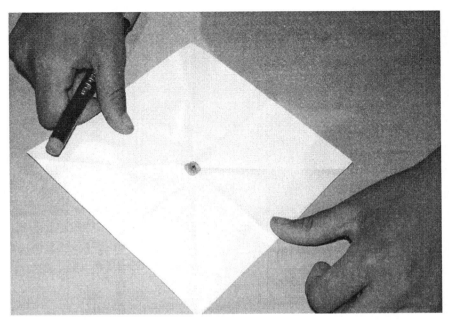

Students follow a sequence in the mandala picture project; here, partners mark centerpoint on square for shared mandala. (Photo: Carmine Tabone)

Proud pair show their mandala to teacher and group. (Photo: Carmine Tabone)

Each pair's work is displayed on group mandala. (Photo: Carmine Tabone)

the paper to Student B, who folds the paper again in half, and now the triangle is even smaller.

- Explain that the squares now have a visible center point. Student B then puts a dot or square in the center spot. Student B then passes the paper back to Student A.
- Guide Student A, who has the paper, to draw a design that will get repeated around the center. (If a shape is outlined, Student A can color it in on that same turn.)
- Guide Students A and B to take turns adding to the mandala and passing it back and forth.

3. Arrange all the mandalas into one large mandala on the large piece of craft paper (approximately four feet by four feet).

- Involve the class in the decision-making process. For a more interesting design, guide students to cut some of the mandalas in half.
- Add designs, using a marker or a paint brush, to tie all of the mandalas together based on suggestions from students. For

example, if a student suggests to add curved lines, draw four or five curved lines with a red marker at points around the group mandala. This helps tie together the mandalas done by pairs into one unified work.

4. Hang the project in a prominent place where other classes or groups can see and appreciate it.

Wrap-Up

1. Discuss how the art project and process demonstrate cooperation in action.

2. Ask students if they have an understanding of why it is important to cooperate with each other when working on a task.

Extensions and Enrichments

1. Demonstrate how to create a word collage or poem.

   - Ask the class to title a mandala that you used during the opening explanation.
   - Divide the class in half. The first group provides a word, phrase, or line. The second group provides the next. The groups take turns creating the group collage or poem.

2. Ask the pairs of students to title their individual mandalas.

   - Guide them to write with Magic Marker the name on the tops of pieces of paper.
   - Coach the partners to take turns providing a word, phrase, or line for their word collages or poems.

3. Hang the word collages or poems around the class mandala in a decorative way. Use the mandala pictures as a backdrop for your storytelling sessions or for any of the stories that you enact.

Story: "The Three Questions"—Russian Folktale (Grades 3–6)

In this Russian folktale, a young prince learns through experience what values in life are important.

A young Russian Prince, feeling a desire to know all about the world, asked his father, the Tsar of Russia, three of the most difficult questions:

- "When ruling a land—or just living in it—what is the greatest thing one can do under the sun?"

- "When is the best time to get something done?"

- "When working with many different people, who is the most important one?"

The Prince also asked his mother, the Queen, and his sister, the Princess (who was studying to become a physician), the same questions. No one in his family knew the answers to these questions.

The Tsar told his son, "I do not know the answer, son, but I will send messengers on foot and horse throughout the land. Whoever returns with the correct answer will be rewarded handsomely."

The responses, many and varied, came back, but none of them were to the satisfaction of the Tsar and the Prince.

The Prince, who was impatient to learn about the world, decided to visit a Hermit, who was thought to be one of the wisest people in the land.

The Tsar said to his son, "You may visit the mountaintop where the Hermit lives. But the Hermit only lets poor people see and talk to him. He does not at all like high and mighty people, such as I may consider myself—and yourself, as well."

So the Prince disguised himself as a peasant and set off on his journey with some guards, who were also disguised as peasants. However, when he reached the mountain, he decided to go on alone to visit the Hermit.

When the Prince got to the top of the mountain, he saw the Hermit fixing up the sides of his hut, making sure the thatches were all secure. The Prince, still disguised of course, approached him and after greeting him kindly said, "If you don't mind, sir, I would like to ask you three important questions. But first let me help you thatch your hut's roof."

This the Prince did while the Hermit rested. After a while, both the Hermit and the Prince were resting on the ground. The Prince thought it a good time to ask the questions:

- "When ruling a land—or just living on it—what is the greatest thing to do under the sun?"

- "When is the best time to get something done?"

- "When working with many different people, who is the most important one?"

The Hermit was polite but did not say anything. The Prince began again to help thatching the hut. After the Prince fixed a large portion of the hut, the Hermit worked on the garden, and the Prince again helped him. This they did under the hot sun.

Finally, after toiling many hours, the Prince put down his garden tools, gently approached the Hermit, and again asked the three questions.

In the middle of the questioning, the Hermit suddenly said, "Listen. Over there, in the forest is the sound of someone running. Do you hear it? There! The shadow of someone running. Do you see?"

Just then, a man with a long beard came out of the woods. He was wounded! He was holding his hands against his stomach, which was all covered with blood. The Prince wasted no time. He carefully cleaned the wound, using used his own shirt to stop the bleeding. The Hermit helped the Prince carry the man into the hut. The man was able to sleep, but the Prince stayed by his side throughout the night, making sure he was alright.

In the morning, the Prince felt relieved that the man was still alive. The man was very weak but managed to whisper to the Prince, "Forgive me—please."

The Prince was startled. "Forgive you? For what?" he said.

The man said, "You don't know this, but I have seen you at the side of your father, the Tsar. I had vowed to take vengeance on him for killing my brother during the last war and taking everything my brother owned and everything I owned."

The Prince listened carefully as the man continued. "When I found out that the Tsar's son was coming up the mountain, I made up my mind to surprise you, but instead of you I ran into your father's guards who recognized me and gave me this wound. I escaped and made my way here."

"If you had not helped me, I would have died for sure," said the man. "You took care of me through the night, giving me life! I'm so ashamed."

The Prince motioned for the man to rest, but he continued: "Now I will be of service to you and your children when you marry. Please, I beg your forgiveness."

The Prince was touched by the plea of the man, a former enemy of his father, to forgive him. The Prince said that he was sorry about what had happened to the man's brother. He vowed that he would ask his father to return all of the man's property. He would ask his older sister, a physician in training, to make sure that the man was completely healed. He promised that his guards would come to the mountain to take the man home. Then the Prince thanked the Hermit and returned to the royal palace, where he recounted to his father, mother, and sister the events of the previous day.

A few days later, the Prince went back to the Hermit. He saw him working in his garden. He decided to ask the questions again.

"You still ask," the Hermit said, "but the questions have already been answered."

"Really?" the Prince exclaimed. "But how so?"

"If you had stopped along the mountain trail and had not continued up to help me with my hut and garden, you would have been attacked by that soldier. Therefore, the best time to get something done was the time you stopped here. The most important person in your life was I, and the greatest thing to do was to help me."

The Prince thought about this and then said, "I think I understand. When the wounded soldier came up here, the best time I spent was helping him by cleaning and dressing his wound, because otherwise he may have died. He was the most important person, and the best thing to do was to help make him healthy again."

"Yes," said the Hermit, "that you did. You now do understand the answers to the three questions you asked. Who you are with is the most important one, and the most important thing in life to do is to serve others, in whatever form that takes."

The Hermit smiled and extended his hand. "Go now, friend," he said. "Remember the people you serve and the happiness you can bring them in the moment. Rule and live in peace."

Act Out the Story

Recommendation: Spread this story enactment over two or three sessions.

Goal: Students will enact and write about a story that deals with exploring life's values.

Materials: None.

Warm-Up With Pantomime

1. Have students form a circle. Ask them if they ever strongly felt the need to know something about a particular aspect of life. Ask for examples of how they felt and what they did about it.

2. Explain that they will be listening to a story about a Prince who wanted to know more about life and who learned some important lessons. They will act out the story using dialogue and pantomime.

3. Have students briefly try out some pantomime activities that will appear in the story—for example, thatching a roof, repairing a house (which some players can become by forming its outline), or working in a garden. Ask, "What tools will you need to repair the house or work in the garden? Can you show us how you use them?"

Development

1. Tell the story.

Focus on Content

2. Conduct a brief discussion on the three questions in the story. Do students agree that these are important questions? Why or why not? Ask them to repeat, in their own words, the questions in the story.

---

3. Flesh out the characters. Ask questions about the Prince: "Where does he live? What does he want? What does he have to do to reach his goals?" Act out a scene in the palace before the story begins. In role, be the Tsar, Queen, or the Prince's sister and find out what each one thinks about life. Ask questions about the Hermit. Ask some students to do a short monologue as the Hermit, regarding why he lives alone. What does he think and feel about his life? They might show him doing some pantomime activities around the hut.

4. Divide the play action into four scenes: the palace, the Hermit's cottage, the palace, and the Hermit's cottage. Discuss what should take place in each scene, who will be in the scene, and why.

5. Divide the class into groups, each one with a Tsar, Prince, Hermit, and soldiers, as well as any other characters in the play.

Focus on Content

6. Assign the roles in each group or ask for volunteers to play them. Have the players improvise the story. Make sure that they have given their characters distinct traits, for example, how they speak, walk, and look.

---

7. Have each group present its version of the story. Afterward, have students write out dialogue for some of the scenes. They may wish to present the play for another class.

Wrap-Up

1. Discuss with the students if they enjoyed acting out the story. Why or why not? Encourage a variety of responses. Were there any parts that were not clear that they would do over?

2. Encourage the groups to reenact or rewrite any of the scenes if they were not clear or interesting.

3. Do the play again at a later time, perhaps adding simple scenery and costumes (see pp. 20–22 for ideas).

Here is an easy-to-follow rubric that you can use if you wish to continue working on your play: *ACTED IT.*

A*ction:* Clear to follow? Too little, too much? Does the play follow a sequence?

C*haracters:* Were they believable, even if they are fantasy characters? Were their feelings expressed? How so?

T*iming:* Did the play's action go too fast or drag? Did actors listen to each other?

E*nvironment:* Did you establish clearly where the action takes place?

D*ialogue:* Was the dialogue clear and believable, and did it fit the characters?

I*magination:* Was the story acted out with imagination? Was it clear, interesting, and worthwhile to act out? Why or why not?

T*eamwork:* Did everyone work together to make the play work? Give some examples.

Extensions and Enrichments

- Conduct a panel called "Experts Answer the Three Questions," in which student panelists discuss what they consider important values to believe in.

- Do the story as a shadow play (see pp. 130–132 for instruction on how to do shadow theater).

- Perform the play for other classes (see tips for making costumes and scenery on pp. 20–22).

Helpful Resources

Stories and Poems

Bloom, Harold. (2001). *Stories and poems: For extremely intelligent children of all ages.* New York: Simon & Schuster.

Brody, Ed. (Ed.). (2002). *Spinning tales, weaving hope: Stories, storytelling, and activities for peace, justice, and the environment.* Gabriola Island, BC: New Society.

Cole, Joanna. (Ed.). (1982). *Best-loved folktales of the world.* New York: Anchor Books / Doubleday.

Hahn, Thich Nat. *The miracle of mindfulness: A manual on meditation.* Boston: Beacon Press, 1987. See Travers (1966) in the following section, Creative Drama.

MacDonald, Margaret Read. (1992). *Peace tales: World folktales to talk about.* Hamden, CT: Linnet Books.

Neile, Caren. *Storytelling for peace.* International Storytelling Center. http://storytellingcenter.net/resources/articles/neile1.htm.

Simms, Laura. (1993). *Making peace—Heart uprising* [Sound recording]. Chicago: Earwig Music.

Ward, Winifred. (1982). *Stories to dramatize.* New Orleans, LA: Anchorage Press.

Creative Drama

Ackroyd, Judith, & Boulton, Jo. (2001). *Drama lessons for five- to eleven-year-olds.* London: David Fulton.

Heinig, Ruth. (1987). *Improvisation with favorite tales.* Portsmouth, NH: Heinemann.

McCaslin, Nellie. (2005). *Creative drama in the classroom and beyond.* Boston: Allyn & Bacon.

Polsky, Milton. (1998). *Let's improvise: Becoming creative, expressive, and spontaneous through drama.* New York: Applause Theatre Books.

Polsky, Milton. (2001). *Improv workshop handbook: The object is teamwork—Creative movement and verbal interaction for students, K–8.* Studio City, CA: Players Press.

Swamp, Chief Jake. (1966, Fall). The peacemaker's journey. *Parabola, 21*(3), 42–46.

Travers, P. L. (1966, Fall). Peace [Special issue]. *Parabola, 21*(3). Contains the Russian story "The Three Wondrous Answers" by Thich Nhat Hanh and "The Peacemaker's Journey" by Chief Jake Swamp.

Review and Move On

As you continue your sessions, remember to

- *Reflect* on the progress that your students have made.

- *Establish* clear and effective signals for starting, facilitating, and bringing to a close the activities.

- *View* your space options in the classroom with an eye to opening up possibilities where exciting things can happen.

- *Investigate* creative ways to expand and deepen techniques in this book, including side coaching and teaching in role.

- *Evaluate* students' involvement in the activities, including meaningful ways for them to assess their own progress.

- *Work* out a strategy for adapting new stories to tell and act out.

CHAPTER THREE
CONFLICT AND CONSEQUENCES

What we do in the world really matters. Like the stone whose impact on a pond sends out a series of ripples from the point of contact, our actions in the world have consequences on those around us. When children or adults act out from frustration, anger, and stress, those around them are profoundly affected. But when children learn to become aware of their emotions and experience how others feel, they are able to reflect on a situation at the point of conflict, thus short-circuiting negative results that might otherwise ensue.

Drama is a powerful, proactive strategy that teaches young people that there are consequences to what they do and that others are affected by their behavior. When students learn lessons through dramatic activity, they try on various roles that show them how to act and react—and how not to act—in difficult situations.

As our Second Chances section reveals (pp. 59–60), drama enactment sheds light on alternative ways of dealing with frustration and tension. When students reflect on the stories that they have enacted, they become open and receptive to think deeply about what they have learned. The dynamic combination of action and reflection helps children take a step back when they are feeling stressed and challenged. Through this process they can make wise choices and learn how to deal effectively with difficult situations.

The stories that we have selected for this section look at various aspects of how unmediated behavior can hurt those around us and destroy relationships with those we care about. For example, in the story "When Frog and Mouse Were Friends," students learn how easy it is to fall out of friendship if the time is not taken to examine all the facts when faced with a problem. Students also experience the selfish behavior of a young man in the "Curse of the Water Monster Creature" and the devastating effect of his selfishness upon the community. "The Quails' Story" examines the meaning of cooperation and compromise and what happens when groups disagree, fight, and decline to work together for the common good.

The stories in this section help students reflect on other important life-examining topics, such as honesty, greed, and deception, and how they negatively and positively affect the relationships of all those involved by how they feel about and treat each other.

More Helpful Tips: Become Drama Detectives—A Nursery Rhyme: "Little Miss Muffet"

Flesh Out the Characters

> Little Miss Muffet
> Sat on a tuffet
> Eating her curds and whey.
> Along came a spider,
> Who sat down beside her
> And frightened Miss Muffet away.

Even this simple nursery rhyme may be easily expanded for playmaking by asking the three *W*s—*who, what,* and *where* (and then *how, why,* and *when*).

Guide students to start thinking as though they are detectives investigating a case. Who is Miss Muffet? What does she look like? How old is she? Where does she live? In a castle? In a hut? What color is her dress? What is a tuffet? Where is she sitting when the spider comes along—in the garden, in her living room, in a school classroom?

Now let's get a little deeper into the story. Ask some character questions. For example, Is Miss Muffet hungry, or doesn't she want to eat her curds and whey? Hey, what are curds and whey, anyway? Do you eat them with your hands or with a spoon? Is she having lunch or supper? So what time of the day or night is it? Is she on a diet, and is that all she can have to eat? Perhaps as she is eating, she is dreaming of having a nice juicy steak instead—or a vegetarian burger? "Let's eat some curds and whey with her *(pantomime this)*."

"What kind of spider comes along? Is it a mother spider looking for her children or a grouchy one with hairs all over his or her body? Does the spider want to be friendly, or is it merely asking for directions? How does the spider move? Where does it come from?" Let's make a spider web to-gether before the story begins *(students touch each other's fingertips and make appropriate sounds)* . . . and so on, until the students and you have developed a small play with a beginning, middle, and end.

Second Chances

How often in life do we wish that we could have done things differently under different circumstances? Or do we wonder about a story—what *if* it had ended differently or what if there were another meeting between the main characters under different circumstances. In creative drama, students have those kinds of opportunities when the time is appropriate.

As the stories in this section show, conflict is a common factor in life. But the stories also show that many unnecessary conflicts in life can be avoided or resolved when people listen carefully to each other, express their feelings clearly, and take the time to communicate to each other the basis of their concerns.

If you decide to redo a story with the purpose of finding a peaceful resolution between adversarial characters in the story, you can do a number of things to help students work through a new scenario that might likely diffuse the conflict. For example, to help their characters, students, in role, might agree to cool off and take some deep breaths, relax, and count to 10; agree to work things out peacefully by talking things over; listen to each other, using *I* statements and brainstorm plans and alternative solutions—keeping on until the one best possible action plan and solution work for the benefit of all concerned.

I statements start with "I feel . . ." *(name the emotion)* ". . . when you . . ." *(describe the behavior)* ". . . because . . ." *(state the effect it has)*. For example, take the little poem story "Little Miss Muffet." Here is what might happen with the help of your coaching the negotiation possibilities.

- Little Miss Muffet goes to Spider's barn for a visit, and Spider is frightened by her at first. Spider says, "I was scared when you came in because I wasn't expecting you and it makes me nervous." They freeze and relax for a moment and make some eye contact.

- They get to become good friends by asking some questions about each other. They work out a plan to help each other as friends.

- Miss Muffet shows Spider how to eat curds and whey.

- Spider shows Miss Muffet how it spins silk.

Any of these possibilities—and any that you and your students can think of—are fun to do and instructive as well, depending on the needs of the class.

Have fun exploring alternative peaceful behaviors with your students through acting out transformative alternative endings of stories. Second chances offer students a lot to think about.

Story: "When Frog and Mouse Were Friends"— United States of America (Grades 3–6)

Why is it important for friends to know the facts about something before starting to argue?

Once upon a time, a mouse and a frog lived together near a woodland pond. They would sleep all day long in their little cottage. But when the night arrived and the moon rose in the evening, they would then come out to sit on their porch and tell each other fairy tales.

One evening Frog took a flower down to the pond to get water. The water was sparkling with stars like precious jewels in some royal treasure house. When Frog saw this, he went back to the house to tell Mouse. "Mouse, come see how rich we are!" Frog cried out.

Together they ran back down to the pond. Mouse could not believe her eyes. Then she fell into thought. "Frog," she said, after awhile, "you and I must take turns to guard our treasure so that no one can steal it."

"You are right," said Frog. So they took turns to watch over the pond until morning. The last watch fell to little Mouse.

Who knows what happened? Perhaps little Mouse dropped off to sleep for awhile, but in the morning there was no sign of the sparkling treasure in the pond.

"Frog!" Mouse cried. "You have stolen our treasure!"

"I?" said Frog angrily. "You are the one who had the last watch. You must have stolen it!" Then Mouse and Frog began to argue so bitterly that in the end they parted company and went to live separately.

What fools they were, for that evening, as the moon crept into the sky, the pond was once again full of stars.

Act Out the Story

Recommendation: This lesson is designed for two or three periods.

Goal: Students will explore, through improvisation and script writing, the topic of friendship—specifically, the disruption of friendship.

Materials: Drawing paper, pencils.

Warm-Up

1. Discuss briefly with students the qualities they look for or value in a good friend.

   - Ask the class what kinds of things friends do together. How would they feel when they do them together?
   - Ask for some examples of why friends might quarrel. What feelings would they express?

2. Tell students that today they will act out a story in which two friends have a fight and that they will explore how the fight might have been prevented.

3. Ask them to imagine that they are each holding a ball. Instruct them to toss it in slow motion to a classmate.

- Coach the students to work with a partner to come up with a sport or hobby that friends do together. Pairs of students take turns demonstrating the activity in pantomime as the rest of the class takes turns guessing what the activity is.

Development

1. Ask students if they can think of an argument that two friends might have had. How could it have been avoided?

2. Explain that today they will be acting out and writing about a friendship that was disrupted because the information they had was misleading.

3. Tell the story in your own words, or hand out copies of the story for the students to read.

4. Discuss why Mouse and Frog have a falling out. Guide students to team up in pairs and improvise the scene where Mouse and Frog argue.

   - Ask, "Why do you think Mouse and Frog argue?"
   - Ask, "How could this argument have been avoided?" Encourage diversity of responses and full discussion. "How could Frog and Mouse have reached for the stars to find out what the real treasure was—perhaps preserving a friendship?"

Focus on Content

5. Ask the students again to come up with one thing that could hurt a friendship or cause a rift between two friends. Guide them to improvise, write about, or draw a picture of the conflict. Invite volunteers to share their work with the group.

6. Guide the class to decide on which one of the situations they would like to work on further. Help students create as a tableau the moment of the conflict. Discuss the tableau with the class and ask students what incidents or actions could have led to this moment.

7. Review possible ways that the two friends in the tableau might resolve their differences. Ask the class to create a second tableau, showing one of these resolutions. Coach students to have the tableau (see pp. 18–20) come alive with the addition of dialogue.

Wrap-Up

1. Discuss how the story of "When Frog and Mouse Were Friends" may relate to similar situations that the students have observed or heard about in their lives.

2. Ask each student to say one word or phrase that he or she learned about taking the time to work through a difficult situation with a friend. Discuss the feelings evoked by the word or phrase.

Extensions and Enrichments

1. Help the class to create a script based on the two silent tableaus, adding action and dialogue.

2. Guide the students to rehearse the scripts in groups of two or three and to show their work to the rest of the class.

3. Play the "Stars" game: Give out a star (made or mimed) every time a student suggests a good or great way to prevent a needless conflict by talking out things. Find a space in class to put the stars.

Story: "The Quails' Story"—Asian Folktale (Grades 3–6)

Sometimes seemingly small conflicts can turn into great disasters.

Long ago there was a Hunter who went into the forest each day to hunt quails. Although quails are small, he was able to catch large numbers of

Third graders practice movement in the class play "When Frog and Mouse Were Friends." (Photo: Ted Rodriguez)

them with his special bird whistle. His whistle sounded like one quail calling to another. And so, when he blew his whistle, any quail within earshot would come flying. When they had gathered together, he would come out from his hiding place and throw a net over them.

He would gather up the net and take the quails back to his wife. She would put each of the quails in a little cage and feed them each day. When the quails grew large enough, the Hunter would take them to the village market. He would sell them and make a good deal of money.

Over time, the flocks of quails grew smaller. One day, a Young Quail said to another quail that he noticed most of his relatives were gone. The other quail, a little wiser and older, explained that in the area there was a Hunter who used a bird whistle and a net to catch quails. The Young Quail became upset and wondered what the quails could do to save themselves from such a fate. The Older Quail thought for some time. Then he suggested that the next time the Hunter used his bird whistle, all the trapped quails should fly up as one and escape.

The Younger Quail thought that this was a great idea. And so, he flew around the forest telling all the quails of this plan.

They did not have long to try it out, for the very next day, the quails in the area gathered when the Hunter blew his whistle. As the quails clustered together wondering who had called them, the Hunter threw his net over them. The Young Quail was ready. "Let's go!" he said. He gave the signal, and all the birds flew together as one to lift the net to a nearby bush with thorns. The quails were free.

For some time after that, the Hunter was unable to capture the birds, for each time he tried, they would fly off together to their freedom.

The Hunter's wife was concerned because they had less to eat. "Don't worry," the Hunter said, "the quails will not continue to cooperate together for a long period of time."

How true these words were. For one day, a number of quails were chatting in the forest. Some of the younger quails bragged, "How strong we are!"

Others said, "Sure, you are strong, but you're not very clever." One thing led to another, and before long the birds were fighting with each other. Suddenly, they heard an inviting quail whistle. They all flew off to see who could be calling them. When they landed, they found themselves covered with a net. One of the quails yelled to another, "Since you are so strong, let's see you lift this net all by yourself."

The other quail said, "Well, if you're so clever, let's see you figure out another way out of here."

And with that, all the quails began to argue and fight with each other. As they fought, the Hunter calmly gathered them up and brought them home. There, his wife put each one in a cage to be fattened up and sold at the market.

Act Out the Story

Recommendation: Spread this story enactment over two or three sessions.

Goal: Students will act out and write about a story that shows how a lack of cooperation between friends can be devastating.

Materials: Copies of the story.

Warm-Up

1. Ask the class, "Have any of you ever had trouble cooperating on something that required teamwork?"

2. Explain that today the class will be acting out and writing about quails who have a tough time working together.

3. Divide students into pairs (Student A and Student B).

    - Ask Student A to shape Student B into a quail searching for food in the forest.
    - Guide Student B to shape Student A into the Hunter hiding behind a tree and blowing the whistle.
    - Coach the students to create the moment as a tableau when the quail is responding to the Hunter's call.
    - Give the pairs the opportunity to show their quail and hunter scene to the rest of the class.

Development

1. Tell the story in your own words, simply but dramatically.

2. Ask the students to write a list of possible things that the quails said to each other when they were responding to the Hunter's whistle. Direct them to share with partners what they have written.

3. Coach a group of five to six volunteers to share this moment.

Focus on Content

4. Direct the partners to improvise a short scene showing two of the quails arguing over who was stronger or more clever.

    - Ask the class what other kinds of things the quails could be arguing over.

5. Ask the students to write the scene of the two quails arguing with each other, with their partners, by passing sheets of paper back and forth until they are finished.

---

6. Guide students to create an improvisational dialogue in pairs.

   - Ask Student As to become reporters who are writing about life in the forest. Ask Student Bs to become the quails who escaped.

7. Coach the class to write a short scene based on the previous verbal dialogue between the reporters and the quails.

Focus on Content

8. Guide three students to create a tableau (see pp. 18–20) of the Hunter's wife feeding the quails after they have been caught.

   - Discuss the tableau that is portrayed and ask the class for suggestions on other possible ways that the tableau could be depicted.
   - Guide the students to create dialogue for this tableau.
   - Ask them to write a short scene of what was just presented. Make sure that they include stage vocal directions, when appropriate.

Wrap-Up

1. Discuss how the story related to situations that the students have observed in their school or community.

2. Guide them to share their writings concerning "The Quails' Story."

Extensions and Enrichments

1. Discuss with the class what other possible scenes they would need to create and write to have a complete play.

2. Continue to work with students on additional scenes, depending on the class's interest.

3. Discuss with them the possibility of creating a short play based on the scenes they wrote to be shared with other classes.

Story: "The Curse of the Water Monster Creature"— Australian Folktale (Grades 3–6)

What can happen when a person in a group does not want to listen to others and a conflict results? What happens when a conflict between people is not resolved? This cautionary story deals with the importance of sending positive messages and the need for cooperation and resolving conflict peacefully.

> Hear our tale
> Of a tragic blunder
> Long ago in the land
> Way "down under."

Yes, our story takes place in Australia, where one day the leader of a village said, "Friends, we need food right away for our village. Soon there will be nothing to eat. Let us go to nearby ponds and bring back fish to feed our families."

A Young Man said, "Let's bring our boomerangs to pass the time on our journey."

But another Villager answered, "No time for that!"

The Young Man said, "There's always time for some fun. Watch what I can do with a boomerang." He threw the boomerang and followed its flight with his eyes as it came back to him. He stuck out his hand and caught it.

The Village Leader said, "I do not feel you should do that now, because we must start the journey quickly and you're taking up valuable time. So let's get on with our journey."

Before the villagers started on their journey, the Young Man's Little Sister said, "Big Brother, bring me back something special."

The Young Man replied, "I will, Little Sister, I will. I promise."

The villagers started their journey. As they walked, the Young Man said, "My feet hurt. Let's rest."

The Village Leader said in a firm voice, "I feel like you're letting us down because you talk too much. Walk on, like the rest of us."

The Young Man threw his boomerang and said that it was fun to do so. "I'm not slowing down the walking," he said.

The Village Leader told the Young Man that he was slowing down the walking and that he should stop playing with the boomerang.

After walking a while, one of the villagers spotted a pool of water and suggested that they stop to fish there. But the Young Man complained that it was too hot to stop. The villagers started to fish, that is, everyone except for one—the Young Man. Another one of the villagers said to the Young Man, "What about you? You're not fishing at all. Help out!"

The Young Man answered, "Why should I do all the work? Let the others do it. I'm going to swim." Some other villagers thought that this was a great idea and joined the Young Man, swimming in the pond. The rest of the villagers worked hard fishing.

After swimming for a while, the Young Man said that he was getting chilly and that he would fish now—but just for a little bit. He baited his fishing line with some raw meat and started to fish in the pond. After a while, he felt a tug on his line. He yelled out, "Oh, look everyone, my line—it's disappearing! It's pulling me down! Help me!"

The Village Leader came to the Young Man's aid, and together they pulled up a big, hulking creature, sort of like a baby rhinoceros or baby alligator.

"Help!" the Village Leader shouted. "Look! It's a baby rhinoceros!"

"No," said another Villager, "it's a baby alligator!"

Another said, "No! It's both! It's half of each!"

The Young Man said, "It's an alligoceros!"

The Village Leader replied, "Oh, no! It's a baby cub of a giant Water Monster Creature! Throw it back into the pond, or the Water Monster Creature will put a curse on all of us!"

The Young Man said, "Not this cute little cub! I promised my Little Sister I would bring back something special to her."

Suddenly a giant Water Monster Creature rose up from the pond and, moaning terribly, waded toward the Villagers. The Young Man kept on throwing his boomerang at the creature, but the boomerang kept coming back to him.

The Village Leader shouted at the young man, "Forget that boomerang! Drop that little cub. Now! Everyone, we must hurry back to the village!"

But the Young Man held on to the cub, determined to bring it back to his Little Sister. "Don't worry," he said. "We're getting closer to our village. I only wish I could fly there like a bird."

Suddenly, there was a sound of thunder. The Village Leader, running with all of the villagers, said, "The sound of thunder! The curse has come!"

Rushing water began to fill up the land, making a hissing sound. There was water—everywhere. The running villagers could only see the tops of trees. One of the villagers cried out, "It's the curse. Water is covering everything!"

Suddenly, a booming echo sound was heard. "Yes, it is my curse. Because you stole my baby from me, may the curse of floods now follow thee!"

The Village Leader turned to the Young Man and said, "See what you've done! Our trip to the pond is boomeranging—turning back on us—just like that silly boomerang of yours—all because of you. You would not listen. Now drop that cub!"

The Young Man answered that he couldn't let go, because the baby cub creature was holding on to him.

The Village Leader shouted for everyone to keep moving. "We'll escape this," he tried to assure them. "Our village is over there. We're almost there!"

When the villagers returned home, the Young Man's Little Sister ran up to her brother and asked if he had brought her anything back. The Young Man handed her the cub. "Isn't it cute?" he asked.

There was no time to answer because suddenly the water began to fill up the whole valley. Everyone was terrified and started to cling to anyone nearby. The Young Man turned to his Little Sister. "We can't escape from this flood. Quick! We'll climb that tree together. Maybe we'll be safe at last."

The Village Leader told the Young Man, "For the last time, drop that cub!"

The Young Man's Little Sister shook her head and began to cry. "Look at my feet," she said.

"Oh, no," the Young Man said, "they're turning into the webbed feet of a bird!"

"You're turning into a bird, too!" Little Sister said in horror.

The Young Man moaned softly, "What did I do? My arms—wings! Our friends—all changed into birds. It's the curse again! The curse of the Water Monster Creature. Or maybe, it's because of me . . . because I didn't listen: I didn't cooperate. I only thought of myself. Now . . . we're all geese."

The Water Monster Creature clomped toward them and snatched her cub from the Young Man's Little Sister. The villagers flew off as geese. The Water Monster Creature carried her baby cub home. She lived in a cave at the bottom of the sea. And the geese? Sometimes when you pass a pond, you can still hear them, speaking in their own language. And what are they saying? Well, that's their language. But this much we know:

> The underwater creature
> With flood and thunder
> Cursed the lives
> Of those who plunder.
> The moral of the tale,
> As it was shown—
> Leave what is not yours
> Alone!

Act Out the Story

Recommendation: This story should be acted out in two or three sessions.

Goal: Students will enact a story that deals with the need for cooperation and resolving conflict between people who act selfishly and those who act for the benefit of the greater good.

Materials: The story "The Curse of the Water Monster Creature."

Warm-Up: Listen to Your Echo

1. Direct players to stand in pairs, facing each other. Guide Player A to say two sentences, for example, "How are you? How do you feel?"

2. Guide Player B to repeat Player A's last sentence and add one line, for example,
   "How do you feel? I'm feeling fine."

3. Explain that Player A then repeats Player B's last line only and adds a line—for example, "I'm feeling fine. I went to the park yesterday."

4. Direct players, repeating the exercise several times, to say one of the lines together in *A BIG BOOMING VOICE* and then to echo it softly several times.

Development

1. Ask students if they know people who think only of themselves. How does that make them feel? What can be done about or for people who think only of themselves?

2. Explain to students that they will act out a story about a selfish person who cares only about himself and, because of this, brings misery to others.

3. Clarify what a boomerang is, namely, a kind of a throwing club that is flat on one side, round on the other. Because of its peculiar shape, it curves in the air when it is thrown, and it returns near to the spot where the sender threw it. The boomerang is indigenous to the country of Australia. You might want the students to find Australia on the map. Ask students to work in pairs and pantomime throwing boomerangs to each other. Have them focus their eyes and hands on the arc of the boomerang's flight pattern.

Focus on Content

4. Tell the story simply and dramatically.

5. Guide students to reflect on the following parts when you tell the story or when the students read it:

- The Village Leader asks the young man not to play with his boomerang on the journey. Conduct, in role as a tribal chieftain, improvisations with students regarding how the Village Leader

---

makes his request to the Young Man. (He sends positive *I* messages of how he feels about the problem caused by the Young Man's behavior: I feel _____ when you _____ because _____.) Ask, "Do you think how the Village Leader makes his request is a good way to act? Why or why not?"

- What promise did the Young Man make to his Little Sister before leaving the village? Ask, "Do you think it is right for the Young Man to hold on to the present he promised his Little Sister? Why or why not?"

- The Village Leader demands, not asks, the Young Man to throw the baby cub back into the pond. Discuss why the Village Leader's tone of voice is different from when he first asked the Young Man to cooperate with the group. Guide the players to take turns being the Village Leader and the Young Man and to act out or write the dialogue regarding their conflict over the baby cub not being returned to its mother.

6. Involve the students to become, with their movements and gestures, the characters in the story as you tell it. All the students can become the same character at the same time as you tell the story, or you can ask them to play the characters in pairs or in small groups (such as the Water Monster Creature and her baby cub).

7. Tell the story again or read it aloud as the students explore becoming the characters in movement and sound (including dialogue) and experimenting with pacing to include movements of the characters—for example, in the beginning of the story, walking from the village to the pond and, at the end, running back to the village in stylized slow motion.

8. Conduct a discussion after the enactment so that students have an opportunity to reflect on what the story means to them. Ask these kinds of questions:

- "Was the Young Man cooperating with the rest of the villagers when he held on to the baby cub? Explain your response."

Students make a tableau to express the essence of the Water Monster Creature in the Australian story "Curse of the Water Monster Creature." (Photo: Carmine Tabone)

- "How do you think the Water Monster Creature felt when her baby was missing?" In role, be a television reporter interviewing the Water Monster Creature and ask the students these kinds of questions: "What do you think the main idea of the story is? Please explain. Would you have made a different ending for the story if you were the author? Can you give an example or two of what you mean?"

9. Invite students to draw, write about, or paint their impressions of the story. Encourage them to discuss why cooperation is important to accomplish certain goals. Invite them to tell some specific experiences in their lives when cooperation worked well—and when it did not work well for them. What did students learn from this story by acting it out?

10. Invite students to discuss how acting out the story required a great deal of cooperation among the players. Encourage a variety of specific examples.

Wrap-Up

Ask the students what they learned about cooperation—and lack of cooperation. Other questions might include the following:

- "Do you think the Young Man was selfish? Why or why not?"

- "How do you think he could have helped his fellow villagers?"

- "What do you think was more important—helping his fellow villagers or just thinking about himself? What feelings were involved in the choices? Why do you say this?"

- "If you had been a villager, what would you have told the Young Man when he did not cooperate? How would you have told him what you felt? Do you think telling how you felt would have made a difference? In role, can you explain your response?"

Extensions and Enrichments

1. Tell the story as the Water Monster Creature—getting across her point of view.

2. Guide students to do the story as a shadow show (see pp. 130–132).

CHAPTER THREE

More Helpful Tips: Writing a Short Play (Grades 3–6)

Goal: Students will retell, in their own words, familiar stories, legends, or myths dealing with themes of living peacefully in the world, whether it is in the classroom, neighborhood, or community. Then they write plays based on the stories.

Materials: Stories that students can adapt into short plays.

Structure Your Play

1. Guide students to choose a situation in which a central character has a problem with another character, involving strong feelings. For example, in "The Curse of the Water Monster Creature," the Village Leader worries that the village will not have enough food and asks that everyone pay attention on the journey to find fish, but the Young Man wants to play with his boomerang and avoid fishing.

2. Help students to know what their central character and opposing character want. The Village Leader wants the Young Man to put the Water Monster Creature's baby cub back into the water, and the Young Man resists and just wants to play.

3. Coach students, "Ask yourselves why your play starts now." The villagers need food to survive. Some of the villagers head off on a journey to find a pond with fish.

4. Make sure that students decide what the dramatic or suspense question is. Will the villagers be able to escape from the Water Monster Creature? There should also be a clear sequence of events. Is something missing? What could be added, deleted, or changed?

5. Have students determine their play's crisis, the point where the central character has to make a choice involving strong feelings. The Village Leader demands that the Young Man throw the cub back into the water.

6. Guide students to determine their play's climax or emotional high point. The irate Water Monster Creature puts a curse on the villagers.

Rehearse Your Play

Coach students to

1. Give their characters distinct vocal, physical, and behavioral traits—for example, the Village Leader is honest, hardworking, persistent, and kind; the Young Man is lazy, careless, persistent, and uncaring.

2. Improvise dialogue that follows structure and fits each character—for example, the Young Man says, "Hold on," "Wait a minute!" "We have time." Dialogue will move the play along.

3. Run through the play several times, preferably with an audience, even if it is a small one.

4. Get feedback. Ask such questions as "Are the characters and their actions clear? Are the dialogue and pantomime natural and believable? Are settings, with appropriate props, clearly established? How? Is there teamwork? Give some examples of how players worked well together."

5. Revise the play, making sure it is interesting, imaginative, and clear.

6. Perform the play. You can perform the play informally in the classroom or more formally in the school auditorium or gym space on special occasions. Coach students to ask themselves questions like these as a staging list.

   - "Are the players' faces clearly visible to the audience, except when hidden on purpose?"
   - "Do the players move naturally from one stage picture to the next using interesting actions and patterns?"
   - "Does each stage picture have a center of attention or clear focal point so that the audience knows where to look? In what ways?"
   - "Is there variety in visual composition on stage? Can you give some examples?"
   - "Can players be clearly heard, even when music is played?"

Wrap-Up

1. Discuss how the drama project and process demonstrate cooperation in action.

2. Ask students if they have a better understanding of why it is important to cooperate with each other when working on a task toward a common goal. Encourage them to give examples.

Extensions and Enrichments

1. Adapt a story that you already know. If you are lucky to have the play published, you must receive permission in writing to use the story from its publisher.

2. Add, if you like, some simple costumes and scenery for your play (see pp. 20–22) if you invite audiences to see it be performed.

Aesop's Fable: "The Goose With the Golden Eggs"— Ancient Greece (Grades 3–6)

How can greed spoil a peaceful farmer's great discovery?

One day a farmer went to the nest of a goose and found a shiny yellow egg there. The farmer was going to throw the egg away because it was extremely heavy and he thought that someone was playing a trick. Instead of throwing the egg away, the farmer took it home and once there noticed that the egg was really golden. Pure gold!

Every day the goose laid a new golden egg, and soon the farmer became rich selling the eggs. Yes, he grew richer and richer, but he also became greedy. Wanting to get all the gold at once, the farmer killed the goose and opened it up, only to find inside the goose—nothing at all.

Moral: Greed often outweighs itself.

Act Out the Fable

Goal: Students act out the fable of "The Goose With the Golden Eggs" in one of the puppetry forms discussed on pp. 80–81.

Materials: The materials needed for enacting the fable in the puppetry form selected.

Warm-Up

1. Divide the class into pairs after they have heard or read the fable, and discuss what it means to them, including what the fable has to do with peace.

2. Ask, "Have you ever wanted too much of something, for example, like too much ice cream or too much television, even though you knew it was not a good idea? How did it feel? What did you do about it?" Tell them that now they will hear a story about a greedy man and what happened to him.

Development

1. Ask, "How old do you think the farmer is? What does he or she look like? At the beginning of the fable, is he or she rich, poor?" Let's try out a short scene before the story begins. You can be one of the farmer's family members, asking the farmer what he or she would do if he or she were rich.

2. Demonstrate to the class one of the puppet forms (discussed on pp. 80–81).

3. Guide pairs of students to design the puppets for the farmer and the goose.

4. Have the students, in their pairs, practice and perform their puppet plays for themselves and then for the class.

5. Design, as an option, a puppet stage using either a table or a cardboard box (with its front and back cut open) placed on a table. If the show is presented in a wide doorway, a curtain can be made that can spread across the opening.

6. Present the fabulous fables for an invited class.

Wrap-Up

Conduct a discussion on how the pairs-only production and the classroom production went. Ask what this fable and its moral have to do with living in a peaceful world.

Extensions and Enrichments

- Guide students to act out some more fables using different kinds of puppets.

More Helpful Tips: Make Simple Puppets (All Grades)

Creating hand puppets is a popular art activity, especially to enact stories with a few characters in nursery rhymes and fables.

Things as Puppets

Use pencils with blunted points, wooden spoons and scoopers, and hands (e.g., "Where Is Thumbkin?") by dressing up fingers with napkins, felt strips, and Magic Markers. Bandanas with holes cut in the middle make excellent colorful costumes.

Finger Puppets

Help students paste on their fingers felt strips that are designed with Magic Markers. These small puppets can also be used in plays that use larger sock puppets.

Bag Puppets

Encourage your class to bring in clean throwaway materials that are suitable for making bag puppets—buttons, straws, ribbons, socks, and cardboard tubing. The young puppeteers first sketch their designs and then complete them with Magic Markers and pieces of construction paper, felt, and cardboard tubing.

Glove Puppets

Guide younger students to cut off the fingers of old but washed gloves for the base; glue on buttons for the eyes and nose; create the head details;

put the first and second fingers in the neck, the third and fourth fingers in one arm, and the thumb in the other arm.

Sock Puppets

Help students begin working with clean socks by stretching socks over their fists. Then help them stretch their imaginations by adding button eyes, felt eyebrows, and other features corresponding to the characters. For example, a piece of red cloth can be sewn into the puppet's mouth and another piece added for the tongue. Fingers go in the toe, and thumb in the heel. Experiment with creating the upper and lower parts of a mouth.

Feet Puppets

Guide students to work with a variation of sock puppets. As they stand behind a partition or screen, coach them to create characters through use of their feet and dressed-up socks. Students walk from one side of the playing area (behind the screen) to the other, showing how their characters would walk.

Ball Puppets

Use a Spalding or Styrofoam ball. You or other adults cut a hole in the middle for the index finger or thumb. The balls should be cut before the students decorate them with Magic Markers.

Rod Puppets

Coach the students to work with flat or rod puppets. Easy to hold, they are like paper doll puppets. They are made simply from lightweight cardstock or paper plates and pasted on to a tongue depressor or a paddle pop stick. If you want the puppet to move in either direction, make two shapes and paste them together with the stick in the middle.

Shadow Puppets

See pp. 130–132 for instructions on how to make and use shadow theater.

More Helpful Tips: Put On an In-Class Radio Show (Grades 3–6)

The advantage of presenting a radio show in your classroom is that the actors do not have to memorize their scripts, so that they can concentrate on working on characterization. It is fun for the students to work together planning the show, assembling the sound effects, and putting on the show for an invited audience. Follow these simple steps.

1. Guide students to rework the story into radio format. For example, here is a sample opening for "The Emperor's New Suit of Armor" (see pp. 83–87).

   NARRATOR 1: Good afternoon. Today, our class will present "The Emperor's New Suit of Armor," based on the story "The Emperor's New Clothes," by Hans Christian Andersen. So long ago that it could almost be yesterday or today, there lived an Emperor—
   (Sound: Royal music)

   NARRATOR 2: —who loved nothing more than to go to war. For no reason or excuse at all. Just to do it. But the people really were tired of war and told him so.
   (Sound: Music out)

   EMPEROR: Some day I will fight in battle—and win. And then when I ride atop my horse, all the people will cheer me.
   (Sound: Cheering crowd)

   EMPEROR: But my armor is so rusty from not going to war all these years. Let's see how my armor looks in the closet.
   (Sound: Closet opening, ruffling of clothes)

2. Guide students to make a list of all the sound effects and props needed, to collect them, and to try them out. Sound effects are just that—the effect is what is important, not how it looks. Footsteps can be made by tapping a piece of wood on another piece of wood. The opening of a door can be the sound of a drawer opening and closing. The ruffling of clothes can be made by crinkling paper. Encourage students to try out the objects that they think will make the proper effect they are looking for.

3. Assign parts. In this case, it is not how the character looks but how the character sounds. Students can play many different parts. Explore with them various voices for the different characters. Discuss character traits and how voices can reveal something about who the characters are. For example, would a character speak slowly, quickly, loudly, or in a whisper? Is the voice raspy or clear? What makes a character sound sinister, likeable, friendly, cold, calculating, or serious? Coach students to have fun with the voices.

4. Coach students to practice saying the characters' speeches, coordinated with the sound effects. They should not overload the show with sound effects. Only those that fit the telling of the story or that establish pertinent moods should be used.

5. Run the show several times. Pacing is everything. Do not allow for dead spaces. Keep the show moving along.

6. Tape-record the show or invite a class in; set up some stands that look like microphones and present your show.

Story: "The Emperor's New Suit of Armor" (Grades 3–6)

Based on the story "The Emperor's New Clothes," by Hans Christian Andersen.

A foolish emperor who thinks only of himself and about war is ridiculed for his vanity.

Once there was an Emperor who loved nothing more than to go to war. But the people were tired of war and told him there was no reason to go to war now. The Emperor promised them that his rule would be peaceful.

But secretly he dreamed about someday leading his troops into battle. And then, sitting proudly atop his horse, he would wave in victory to the cheering people in the capital square. But without the prospect of war, his suit of armor was now getting rusty from lack of use.

One day, two tailors who were twins—one brother and one sister—came to the capital city, where the Emperor resided. He learned that they were the best tailors in the land and could make any kind of clothes desired, as if by magic. The Emperor summoned them immediately to his palace.

"Make me a new suit of armor, one that is very special," the Emperor commanded them.

"We normally deal with cloth," one of the twins said. "But, yes, we can make anything,'" the other twin said.

"In the event that I have to lead my troops again, I want to have the most fantastic suit of armor ever devised. See to it that you get started immediately."

The two tailors bowed low to the Emperor. "As you desire, sire—to show you off as you so highly deserve," they said, bowing again.

"I will send along all your supplies, pliers, sheers, hammers—and, of course, all the finest silver and gold metals and jewels of any kind you ask for. Now go to the special room I have prepared for you."

As soon as they got to their special room, one twin blurted out, "Do you know how to make a suit of armor from gold and silver?"

"No."

"Neither can I, but we'll tell His Majesty that we can do it—and get to keep the gold and silver for ourselves—and this is how we'll do it," he added, whispering into his twin's ear.

The twins thought it was a great plan, sure to fool anyone.

When the Emperor visited the tailors, they said to him, "What do you think of the metallic pants we have just made over there on the table?"

The Emperor looked at the table but saw nothing, so instead he just nodded his head slightly and smiled.

"We thought you would greatly like it," said one of the twins. And the other said, "The suit of armor we are making for you is not only very strong, but it is also extremely light, so light, in fact, you can hardly feel it."

"I see," said the Emperor. But he didn't see anything.

"And, oh, Your Highness," one of the twins said, "we have reworked the materials you gave us with a special magical substance so that the suit of armor will be invisible to anyone who is unfit for their job—or is just plain foolish. Now, then, what do you think of the pants we have made so far, Your Highness?"

The Emperor thought to himself, "Am I not fit for my job as ruler of the land? Am I a foolish person?" Out loud he answered the twins, "Wonderful! Wonderful! Keep up your terrific work, and I will send you more gold and silver metals—and jewels, too."

The Emperor returned to his royal bedroom. He was beside himself with joy. "This is great," he said to himself. "Not only will I look wonderful in my new suit of armor, but I will be able to tell at once who in my court is not qualified to hold office. I'll also be able to immediately tell the difference between those who are smart and those who are stupid."

Soon everyone in the capital was talking about the Emperor's fabulous new suit of armor. The Emperor himself was curious about its progress but thought it would be a good idea to first send his Top General to make a report.

When the Top General arrived at the work studio of the tailors, he saw them, sheers and pliers in hand, cutting and bending—shaping—something in the air. But what was it? The Top General saw nothing, nothing at all.

"Do you like it, O Great Commander? The shirt of armor for His Majesty? Look here, the swirls of sun we have put on the gold. And, look, see the beautiful impressions of the moon we have made on the silver metals. And connecting the sun and moon, behold these beautiful jewels."

The Top General, of course, could not see a thing. He thought to himself, "Am I not fit for my job? Or am I just plain stupid?"

"Oh, the metallic shirt is just so beautiful. Perfect to match the pants!" he said, pointing toward the table.

"You mean here hanging right in front of you?" asked one of the twins.

"Of course, of course," the Top General sputtered, "the pants hanging right in front of me. So beautiful! I will tell the Emperor immediately."

"And if you don't mind letting His Majesty know that we can use some more gold and silver—for the head visor and shoes, you know. Thanks!"

The Emperor, of course, sent them more gold and silver, which they immediately put in their knapsack and hid in the closet.

More and more of the Emperor's ministers of high state came to see for themselves the fantastic suit of armor, and each—wishing to hold on to his or her job—did not admit that there was absolutely nothing there of armor to see.

CHAPTER THREE

The twin tailors pretended to work on the suit of armor the night through. People knew that, because the light from 16 candles was seen through a slit in the door.

The next day, when the Emperor heard that the suit of armor—from head to feet—was completed, he decided to see for himself the wondrous completed product. He asked for his Top General and other ministers of state to accompany him to the tailors' workroom.

Pointing to the table in front of them, one twin exclaimed, "There it is; hope you like it, Your Highness!" Then the twins pretended to hold it up for the Emperor to see better. "So light, so light. But still so strong," the twin tailors said proudly.

The Emperor was careful to avoid straining his eyes because, of course, he saw nothing except air and space. But he thought to himself, "I'm fit for my job. I'm not stupid," and then he said very loudly, "Great! Fabulous! Fantastic!"

And the Top General and high ministers in the room immediately echoed in great chorus, "Great! Fabulous! Fantastic!"

"I hereby dub you both Most High Royal Tailors of the Land. And you will march by my side when the parade begins in just a few minutes."

"Thank you, Your Highness. But we must make haste to another kingdom that is expecting us. But we are sure the crowds will adore you and your new suit. And, look, we have also made a visor for your horse's head, a body suit of armor, and knee protectors."

"Thank you," said the Emperor, "and now I am ready to get into my suit of armor."

"First, sire, take off all your clothes, and we will help you into your new suit of armor."

With everyone else staring ahead and at the same time strongly suppressing their smiles for fear that they would lose their jobs or look just plain foolish, the Emperor took off all his clothes, except for his long underwear.

The twins pretended then to carefully help him put on his new suit of armor. Everyone in the room gasped in awe. "How beautiful!" they said, almost in one voice.

"Look in the mirror, Your Highness, to see how wonderful you look," one of the twins said.

The Emperor did so and said he agreed that, indeed, his new suit of armor was wonderfully special. Everyone else in the room quickly agreed.

Then, the twins, bowing, said, "We have all our tools in our knapsacks. Good luck, Your Majesty, you look fantastic." And with another bow, they swept out of the room and ran for their lives out of the city.

The Emperor, sitting proudly atop his horse, waved happily to the cheering crowd along the parade route. Everyone *oohed* and *ahhed* at the new suit of armor, pointing to the swirling golden suns and silver moons and glowing inlaid jewels.

But then a child in the crowd said to her mother, "The Emperor has nothing on."

Soon enough, there was a groundswell of murmuring throughout the crowd. "She's right, the Emperor has nothing on except his long underwear!"

Of course, the Emperor, now his face turning the color beet red, realized this, too. He knew that he could not now talk about going to war. He could not talk at all—he was too embarrassed to do anything but continue along the parade route, his head still held high but his spirit very low as the ripple of laughter along the parade route got louder and louder.

Act Out the Story as an In-Class Radio Show

Recommendation: This story enactment may involve two or three sessions of preparation.

Goal: Students will write and enact a story in a radio format.

Materials: Objects for sound effects.

Warm-Up: Make Sounds

1. Have students form a circle or straight line. Have the radio players take a big, big yawn. Then, as a way of relaxing, they can slowly and gently roll their heads around to the right and to the left and, like rubber duckies, scrunch their shoulders up to their ears and do some arm windmills in slow motion.

2. Have students call out their names or zip codes, first in a small voice, as if cut from fine crystal glass; then in a great, big, loud voice; and, finally in their own, normal voices or in the voices of the characters whom they will play in the radio show.

3. Coach students to do some tongue twisters, such as "Peter Piper picked a peck of pickled peppers" or "Many mumbling mice making midnight music in the moonlight. Mighty nice!" Make up some of your own alliterative gems. If there is time, the students can tell some brief group stories right on the spot, following the instructions on pp. 90–91, or they can retell the story of "The Emperor's New Suit of Armor."

Development

1. Tell the story or have students read it aloud.

Focus on Content

2. Flesh out the characters. Ask such questions about the Emperor as "How old is he? What does he look like in the story? How does he walk and talk? What does he want in the story? Why?" In role, be a newspaper reporter and ask the Emperor all kinds of nosey questions. In pairs, coach the students to imagine they are the twins, discussing how they will trick the Emperor. What do the twins look like? How do they talk and move?

---

3. Play the game "Inner Voices." When the yes-men and yes-women say how much they think the suit of armor is terrific, place your hand over their heads. As an aside or inner voice (low but audible, perhaps mixed with shame), they must tell the truth about what they see (or really do not see).

4. Coach students to rewrite the story as a radio play (see pp. 82–83).

5. Guide them to collect and organize sound effect props on a table, preferably on the stage right side of the classroom. The sound effects made by students (no more than two at the table) are an important part of the radio ensemble. They should be visible to the audience, and the audience should clearly see

what they do. But sound effects should never overwhelm the production but instead be interwoven with the rest of the script in a natural, organic way.

6. Supply some real or made-up microphones that stand up. At the same time, provide for at least one tape recorder to copy the show.

7. Make sure that you have a radio show student director and a student stage manager to keep things moving at a good pace. Above all, avoid dead space. Keep the show moving. Students should come up to the microphone before the current speaker has completed his or her line. This takes practice, so take time to work on this aspect of the pacing. Guide students to speak clearly and to stay in character at all times.

Wrap-Up

1. Guide students to discuss the production: What worked? What didn't? Why? Have students give some examples. What did they learn from the experience? Do they think that the Emperor was really interested in peace—or just in himself? Ask them to explain.

2. Redo parts of the radio production that need more work. Take the time to correct things that have not worked. Encourage patience and teamwork.

3. Do another production of the show as a nonradio play, and when it is ready, invite another class to see it.

Extensions and Enrichments

- Encourage students to adapt more of their favorite stories dealing with war and peace.

- Encourage them to write the stories in a radio format and to act them out.

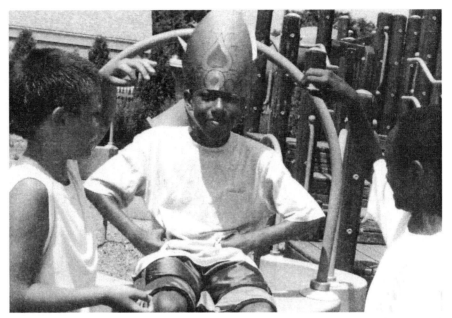

The clever weavers entice the haughty Emperor with their invisible armor in the story "The Emperor's New Suit of Armor." (Photo: Carmine Tabone)

More Helpful Tips: Make Up a Group Story Right on the Spot

> *Goal:* Students will create stories improvisationally as a group.
> *Materials:* None.

1. Explain or model how the game is played. Each group of players (about eight) form a horizontal line. The first player in the line starts the story by saying "once"; the second player quickly adds "upon"; and the next player in line adds "a." Somehow, the story must incorporate an object and a place, suggested by the audience.

2. Guide players, first time around, to add only one word to the growing story, reaching the player at the end of the line. Then the story continues nonstop, with the first player in line saying the next word. In turn, the second player, the third player, and so on, each contribute a word. The second time around, each

consecutive player adds one or more sentences to the story as it grows and grows. The story may or not make sense. It doesn't have to. It should just be kept going and going for a couple of minutes.

3. Coach, "Stand shoulder to shoulder. Make sure that you can be heard by all the players on your line, especially by the players at the end of the line. If you get stuck, say 'but' or 'so' or 'then,' and so on." Make sure that players tell the story in the past tense and use "he," "she," "they," "it," instead of "I" and "we."

Wrap-Up

- Encourage students to create on-the-spot stories motivated by different themes—for example, a scary story, an adventure story, a story from history or current events, a peaceful story, and so on.

Extensions and Enrichments

- Once the students get the hang of how to do this exercise, they can experiment by adding gestures and human-made sound effects.

- Invite them to write down one of the stories or to adapt the stories that they made up while on the line.

Helpful Resources

Educators for Social Responsibility. http://www.esrnational.org. A source of curriculum materials, books, and teacher training programs that focus on issues of peacemaking and conflict resolution.

Hudson, Ilene, & Judson, Marilyn. (1977). *Simple folk instruments to make and play.* New York: Simon & Schuster.

Kreidler, William J. (1984). *Creative conflict resolution: More than 200 activities for keeping peace in the classroom.* Glenview, IL: Scott, Foresman.

Roberton, E. Jean. (1979). *Hans Andersen's fairy tales*. New York: Schoken Books, 1979.

Schechner, Richard. (1973). *Environmental theatre*. New York: Hawthorn Books.

The 1000 page book of stories. (1985). New York: Longmeadown Press.

Way, Brian. (1971). *Development through drama*. New York: Humanities Press.

Zipes, Jack. (1992). *Aesop's fables*. New York: Signet Classics.

Zipes, Jack. (2004). *Speaking out: Storytelling and creative drama for children*. New York: Routledge.

CHAPTER FOUR
BULLYING AND TEASING

We believe that all children should be grounded in positive social values. Stories accompanied by drama activities can teach children many positive values, such as how to be honest, how to share, how to place boundaries on their behavior, how to stand up to what is wrong, how to be trusting or wary of others (depending on the situation), and how to be a good friend. These values are crucial to the building of a society that can function not only well but peacefully. In such a society individuals need to treat each other with respect without resorting to violence to resolve disagreements that express pent-up aggression.

Bullying is one of the first indicators of future violent behavior among young people. Social scientists characterize bullying as unprovoked abuse by one or more children to inflict physical pain or psychological distress on another child on repeated occasions. Such children, "bullies," are unaware of, or do not care about, the effects of their behavior on others.

Common sense and firsthand experience tell us that being the victim of bullying is a humiliating and damaging ordeal. From an educational point of view, teasing and bullying are harmful and may create a classroom climate of fear that affects a child's ability to learn and a teacher's ability to teach.

Interactive drama activities can provide teachers with strategies to help students gain new perspectives that can enhance the social climate in the classroom. Acting out and writing about stories such as "Beetle and Rat" and "Swimmy" and "Rosie's Story" offers students an emotional

93

experience that fosters empathy, trust, and compassion for others—the very qualities that bullies lack. A Native American folk saying asks, "Do not judge me until you have walked a mile in my moccasins."

This section reaches out for that kind of understanding.

Story: "The Three Billy Goats Gruff"—English Folktale (Grades K–2)

How do three Billy Goats work together and use their brains to outwit a mean Troll?

There once were three Billy Goats, and their family name was Gruff. The grass they ate on the meadow was getting very scarce. The oldest and biggest goat told the other two that they would have to go over a wooden bridge to cross the river. There, on the other side, was more grass they could eat. The problem was that under the bridge there lived a mean, ugly Troll who thought that he owned the bridge and wanted to eat anyone who was crossing over the bridge.

The youngest Billy Goat went first. "Trip trap! Trip trap!" went the bridge.

"Who's that tripping over my bridge?" the Troll roared in a loud, angry voice.

"It's only me," said the little Billy Goat in a tiny voice. "I'm trying to go over the bridge to get to the other side to eat some grass."

"Is that so?!" the Troll roared. "Well, I'm going to gobble you all up!"

"Oh, don't do that," the little Billy Goat said in a tiny voice. "My brother is much bigger, and you'll have more to eat. So wait for him."

"Go back and tell him to come here!" the Troll roared.

So then the bigger brother Billy Goat went across the bridge.

"Trip, trap! Trip, trap!" creaked and groaned the bridge.

"Who's that tripping over my bridge?" the Troll bellowed. "I'm going to gobble you all up!"

"No, don't do that," the second Billy Goat Gruff cried out. "Wait for my bigger brother. He's the biggest goat of us all, so you'll have the biggest meal of all."

"Tell him to come here," the Troll said, licking his own lips and laughing with glee.

So the third Billy Goat Gruff went to cross the bridge.

"Trip, trap! Trip, trap!" went the bridge, creaking and groaning very loudly.

"Who's that tramping over my bridge?!" the Troll roared.

"It is I—the biggest goat on my way to eat some grass!" the Billy Goat said in a very loud voice.

"Well, I'm going to gobble you all up!" roared the Troll.

The third Billy Goat decided to use his brain power to scare and confuse the Troll—with words.

"No, you're not going to gobble me up," said the third Billy Goat Gruff, "because I have horns and hoofs—hoofs and horns—horns and hoofs!"

The Troll was so scared of the third Billy Goat's loud voice saying the words over and over, that he fell right into the river.

Then the third Billy Goat called for his two brothers to make their way over the bridge. And all three went over the bridge, and they never heard from the Troll again.

Snip, snap, snout. This tale is told out!

Act Out the Story

Goal: Students will work together to act out a limited-action story to show how working together can help to outwit a bully.

Materials: The story.

Warm-Up

1. Ask, "Have any of you ever had to deal with a bully who was mean and scary? What happened—or didn't happen—and how did it all work out?"

2. Explain that today they will act out a story about a selfish and mean monster, a Troll. (Explain and perhaps show a picture of it from the book.)

3. Tell them that they are going to create some things that appear in the story.

- Coach them to make "mean masks" by stretching their faces in different ways (no using fingers, please!) and then showing their mean faces to a partner.
- Guide children to make a group bridge, sitting down or standing up, with two parallel lines facing each other and with only the palms or tips of their fingers touching.

Development

1. Tell the story in your own words or read this version.

2. Flesh out the main characters.

Focus on Content

- Ask questions about the Troll. "Why is he so mean? What's he doing under the bridge? What does he want? Why does he want it?"
- Act out a scene of Trolls before the story begins, as a teacher-in-role, perhaps as Uncle Troll finding out what the Troll is doing.
- Ask questions about the Billy Goats Gruff. "How are they alike? How are they different? What do they want?"

- Become a teacher-in-role character, playing a television reporter, and act out scene with the three Goats to find out how they intend to get the new grass to eat.

3. Tell the story again as students act it out, becoming all the characters and environments. Introduce vocabulary words such as *hoof* and *horn*, *groaning* and *creaking*.

4. Pay special attention to the ending. Incorporate the words *hoofs* and *horns*. Guide a student to play the third Billy Gruff, who is repeating the words *hoofs* and *horns* over and over while another student, playing the Troll, falls (in slow motion) into the river, which is played by the rest of the students.

Wrap-Up

- Assess the enactment—what students liked, what worked well, what parts they would redo.
- Ask, "During the acting out of the story, was the Troll mean enough, the goats scared enough? Why or why not?"
- Ask, "How did the Billy Goats use their heads (not only horns but brains) to work together to outwit the Troll? How so?"
- Ask, "After the story's ending, what did the Billy Goats do?" Encourage varied responses.

Extensions and Enrichments

Suggest that students draw a scene from the enactment.

Second Chances

> ### Focus on Content
>
> - Ask these "what if" kinds of questions: "What if the three Billy Goats Gruff and the Troll could meet again? Why would they be meeting—and where? Would they meet accidentally or would it be planned? If planned, who would ask for the meeting? Why? Is it possible that they all could be friends? What would happen for this to come true?" Guide students to act this part out.
> - Guide students to make an outline, verbal or written scenario (see pp. 121–123) of what happens. Act out the story again and discuss it, paying special attention to how second chances can lead to a peaceful resolution.

Story: "Beetle and Rat"—Amazonian Folktale (Grades 3–6)

Can a friend help another friend who is being teased?

Once upon a time, long ago, when animals could still speak and before most of the animals had colors, there lived deep in the Amazon jungle a Beetle and a Rat. Now Rat had a nice warm gray coat, but Beetle was very plain. So every day when they saw each other, Rat made fun of Beetle and teased her. Beetle was very quiet about all this.

By the way, there is also a Parrot in our story. Parrot was one of the few creatures that had colors at this time. In fact, Parrot had an array of beautifully colored feathers. Every day Parrot watched from the top of a tree as Rat picked on Beetle.

Parrot wondered if there was some other way that Beetle and Rat could relate to each other than to have Rat always teasing and bullying Beetle. So Parrot decided that he would ask Beetle and Rat if they would like to race each other. He offered the winner of the race its choice of any colors for its covering. Rat thought that this was a great prize and was sure that he would win the race. Beetle wasn't so sure but was willing to go along with Parrot's idea. They all agreed that they would start in the forest near Parrot's tree and that the finish line would be at the end of the village. They agreed to have the race when they would all be rested, early the next morning.

So the next morning the race was held. At Parrot's signal, Rat scurried off into the forest, leaving Beetle way behind. On the way, Rat stopped for a while and thought about all the great colors that he would select for his beautiful, furry coat. After he decided, he hurried off to collect his prize, but when Rat arrived at the end of the village, he saw Beetle sitting in the shade of a tree. Rat was absolutely furious. He began to jump up and down and shout. "How did you get here before I did?" he screamed.

"Well," said Beetle, "I flew here."

Rat had not known that Beetle could fly, so he went to Parrot to complain. Parrot explained that no one had said Beetle could not fly.

"But I didn't know Beetle could fly," said Rat.

"I am sorry," said Parrot, "but you shouldn't have judged Beetle by how she looked." Rat was furious and huffed off into the forest not to be seen again for a long time. Then Parrot gave Beetle a wide array of colors. And that is why to this day, the beetles of the Amazon forest are covered in reds, greens, yellows, and blues. But rats are just plain gray.

Act Out the Story

Recommendation: This lesson is designed for two or three sessions.

Goal: Students, through improvisation, reflection, and script writing, will become aware of how the victim of a bully can get help.

Materials: Copies of the story "Beetle and Rat."

Warm-Up

1. Ask the class, "Have any of you ever heard about someone who is a bully? What is that person like? How does that person make his or her victims feel?"

2. Explain that today they will be working on a folktale from the Amazon that is about a relationship between a bully and a victim and the feelings they experience.

Development

1. Tell the beginning of the story, or hand out copies of the story for the students to read.

    Once upon a time, long ago, when the animals could still speak and before most of the animals had colors, there lived deep in the Amazon jungle a Beetle and a Rat. Now Rat had a nice warm gray coat, but Beetle was very plain. So every day when they saw each other, Rat made fun of Beetle and teased her. Beetle was very quiet about all this.

2. Provide writing and improvisational opportunities such as the following:

    - Ask students to say or write a list of possible things that Rat might say to Beetle and a second list of what Beetle might be thinking in response.
    - Direct them to share with partners what they have written.
    - Discuss with the students what words they would use to describe Beetle and Rat. Guide students to make two lists on the board: one of words describing Beetle; the other, describing Rat.

Focus on Content

3. Create an improvisational dialogue with the class.

- Tell the students that they are Beetle's friends and that you will play Beetle.
- Discuss what Beetle might have said to her friends about Rat and how Beetle's friends might have responded. Make sure that they are clear about Rat's and Beetle's feelings about what is going on.
- Guide students, working in pairs, to create the dialogue. Sample dialogue:

  BEETLE: I am really tired of Rat picking on me so much. I feel so angry.

  FRIENDS: Why do you let Rat speak to you like that?

  BEETLE: I guess I'm afraid of him. He is smarter than I am and bigger, too.

  FRIENDS: Maybe we can talk to him for you.

  BEETLE: That might make it worse.

---

4. Coach the class to write a short scene based on the previous verbal dialogue between Beetle and her friends. Make sure that they keep the dialogue in character and that the dialogue advances the story.

5. Tell students the next part of the story or hand out copies of the story for them to read.

   By the way, there is also a Parrot in our story. Parrot was one of the few creatures that had colors at this time. In fact, Parrot had an array of beautifully colored feathers. Every day Parrot watched from the top of a tree as Rat picked on Beetle.

6. Guide three students to create a tableau (see pp. 18–20) of this moment from the story. The tableau can come alive with students speaking their thoughts.

   - Discuss the tableau that is portrayed, and ask the class for suggestions on other possible ways that the scene could be depicted—for example, the direction in which Beetle faces might be altered. The expression on any of the characters' faces might be changed.

- Ask students to suggest possible dialogue for Parrot. What feelings are expressed?
- Guide them to write the short scene just presented. Make sure that they include, when appropriate, stage and vocal directions.

7. Tell the next part of the story, or hand out copies of the story for them to read.

Parrot wondered if there was some other way that Beetle and Rat could relate to each other than to have Rat always teasing and bullying Beetle. So Parrot decided that he would ask Beetle and Rat if they would like to race each other. He offered the winner of the race its choice of any colors for its covering. Rat thought that this was a great prize and was sure that he would win the race. Beetle wasn't so sure but was willing to go along with Parrot's idea. They all agreed that they would start in the forest near Parrot's tree and that the finish line would be at the end of the village. They agreed to have the race when they would all be rested, early the next morning.

Focus on Content

8. Create with the class a scene of Beetle having second thoughts about the race.

- Speak to the class as if you are Beetle and they are Beetle's friends.
- Explain, as Beetle, to your friends the concerns that you have about tomorrow's race.

---

9. Tell the next part of the story, or hand out copies of the story for students to read.

So the next morning the race was held. At Parrot's signal, Rat scurried off into the forest leaving Beetle way behind. On the way, Rat stopped for a while and thought about all the great colors that he would select for his beautiful furry coat. After he decided, he hurried off to collect his prize, but when Rat arrived at the end of the village, he saw Beetle sitting in the shade of a tree. Rat was absolutely furious. He began to jump up and down and shout. "How did you get here before I did?" he screamed.

"Well," said Beetle, "I flew here."

Rat had not known that Beetle could fly, so he went to Parrot to complain. Parrot explained that no one had said Beetle could not fly.

"But, I didn't know Beetle could fly," said Rat. "I am sorry," said Parrot, "but you shouldn't have judged Beetle just by how she looked." Rat was furious and huffed off into the forest not to be seen again for a long time. Then Parrot gave Beetle a wide array of colors. And that is why to this day, the beetles of the Amazon forest are covered in reds, greens, yellows, and blues, but rats are just plain gray.

Wrap-Up

1. Discuss if the characters improved their relationships with each other as the story progressed.

2. Discuss how the story relates to situations that the students have observed in school or community situations.

3. Discuss the possibility of students creating a short play based on the scenes they wrote for other classes.

Extensions and Enrichments

1. Explain to the class that this Amazonian story ends at the point they heard but that you have another possible ending: *Months later, Rat sent a note to Beetle.*

   - Ask the class to imagine what is in the short note from Rat to Beetle and to write it.
   - Create a small playing space where volunteers can sit and enact the scene where Beetle reads Rat's note aloud.

Creating a forest environment for the Amazonian folktale "Beetle and Rat." (Photo: Milton Polsky)

- Ask students to write a scene showing how Beetle reacted to the note and what might have happened when Rat returned to the village. For example, Beetle might be very indignant that Rat wants to return, so she organizes the other animals in the forest to keep Rat out. Or Beetle might be willing— despite the pleas of her friends not to do so—to forgive Rat and welcome him back.

2. Discuss what feelings and words might be used to describe Beetle and Rat at this point in the story.

   - Guide students to make two lists on the board: one of words describing Beetle; the other, Rat.
   - Discuss what changes have occurred in the characters since the beginning of the story.
   - Explore with students what these descriptions reveal about the relationship of bullies and their victims.

Story: "Rosie's Story"—United States of America (Grades K–3)

Adapted from the picture book Rosie's Story, *by Martine Gogoll.*

What happens when teasing someone about how she looks results in hurt feelings?

Have you ever thought that you looked different from everyone else?

This is the story of a little girl named Rosie who happened to look different from everyone in her family. Rosie had red hair and freckles. Her parents, brothers, and sisters, even her grandparents, did not. They all had different-colored hair. Rosie was very unhappy because she wanted to look like everyone else.

Fortunately, everybody in her family thought that she was beautiful. Her parents, her grandparents, and her brothers and sisters all loved her. They had pictures of her throughout the house. Still, Rosie felt out of place. She just hated her red hair and freckles.

When Rosie was eight, her family moved to another town. Her new class in school was made up of children whose hair was a different color from Rosie's. Some had blond hair, some brown, some black. But none of them had red hair and freckles like Rosie. The children in her new class made fun of her red hair by calling her such names as Carrot, Firecracker, and Strawberry Shortcake.

When she heard these names, Rosie thought to herself, *I really hate my red hair and freckles*. Rosie's parents couldn't understand how she felt. They told her all the time how much they loved her, her red hair and her freckles.

"Don't worry, the children at school soon will tire of their teasing," her parents told her. But that was not the case. Her classmates kept on calling her names every day.

They said things to her like "Let's get away from her; her hair is on fire." Then they would all laugh.

Every night Rosie would try to scrub the red hair from her head and rub the freckles off her body. No use, they would not go away.

One day during writing class Rosie's teacher, Mrs. Clark, said, "Children, I want you all to go home tonight and put together a picture story-book for a contest the school is holding."

Later that day, Rosie went home and tried to put together her story-book. She sat at her desk trying to come up with ideas. But the more she thought, the sadder she grew, until she just sat there crying. When her mother came into her room and asked her what was wrong, Rosie explained that she had to write a story but just couldn't do it. Her mother suggested that she write about how she was feeling. Rosie didn't like the idea, but after some time, she came up with a story about a little boy named Rusty who had red hair and freckles.

The next week during writing class, the children began to take turns reading the stories they had written. One story was funny, another was scary, and another was mysterious. The children loved all the stories.

Finally, it was Rosie's turn. She read her story softly. The class was quiet. At the end of the story Mrs. Clark told Rosie how much she loved the story. She explained how the story reminded her of when she was a girl. Mrs. Clark said that when she was in school, the children in her class used to make fun of her because she was so skinny.

Some of the children in the class then raised their hands and said things like "A few years ago I was very heavy, and other kids used to call me 'Dumpling' and laugh at me."

A girl said that she liked to dance but that the boys would always make fun of her. Another said, "When I had to start wearing glasses, the kids in my class used to call me 'Four Eyes.'"

Rosie's teacher then discussed with the class how easy it is for people to hurt each other's feelings. She also explained that each and every one of us has something about us that others could pick on, if they wanted to.

When Mrs. Clark finished the discussion, she announced that it was time to vote on which story the children liked the best. All of the children wrote the name of their favorite stories on pieces of paper and gave them to Mrs. Clark. Rosie's teacher counted up the votes. In a landslide the children had voted for Rosie's story.

Act Out the Story

Recommendation: This story can be done over the course of two or three sessions.

Goal: Students will better understand the importance of being sensitive to other's feelings.

Materials: Copies of the story.

Warm-Up

1. Explain that you are going to read to the class a story about a little girl who was unhappy about the way she looked.

2. Ask the students to listen carefully so that they will be able to play the parts of some of the people in the story.

Development

1. Read the story to the students up to the end of the second paragraph, *She just hated her red hair and freckles.*

2. Ask for volunteers to come up to the front of the classroom to portray Rosie's family. Include her parents, grandparents, sisters, and brothers. In role as a visiting relative, ask the family members why Rosie is so unhappy these days. Find out if she has always been this way. Explore what the family likes about her. Thank the students for being willing to volunteer.

3. Read the story to the students up to the end of the eighth paragraph, *Then they would all laugh.*

4. Place an empty chair in front of the class. Ask the children what object they could place on that chair to represent Rosie. Do not choose one of the students to play the part but rather some inanimate object.

5. Ask for five volunteers to pose around the chair as characters from that moment when Rosie is being teased.

6. Ask the class for some of the thoughts and feelings that Rosie might be having at this moment. As each of these thoughts and feelings are shared, repeat them in the first person while standing behind the chair that represents Rosie—for example, "I am feeling very scared right now" and "Why are people picking on me?"

Focus on Content

7. Discuss with the class how Rosie is feeling. Ask the students what they, in role as her friends, would like to say to Rosie.

8. Ask the class how they think the people who were teasing her felt at that moment. Ask the students what they, in role as her friends, would like to say to those who are picking on Rosie.

9. Thank the children who were willing to play the people who taunted Rosie. Remind the class that they were just playing a role and were not the people in the story.

---

10. Read the rest of the story to the children. Discuss what some of the children who had teased Rosie might want to say to her after they heard her story.

Wrap-Up

Invite the students, depending on age level, to either write a letter to Rosie or draw a picture for her. Have them write or draw in role as if they were the children who had teased Rosie and now want to apologize.

Extensions and Enrichments

1. Make two sunbursts on the chalkboard.

   - In the center of one circle write, "Ways we are different." Record the student responses on the rays emanating from the sunburst. Discuss briefly the many ways that people are different.
   - In the second circle write, "Ways we are the same." Record the student responses on the rays emanating from the sunburst. Discuss briefly the many ways that people are the same.

2. Create a handout on an 8½-by-11 sheet of paper with a circle in the middle and flower petals around the outside of the circle to form a daisy. Have each student make a self-portrait of himself or herself in the circle. In the surrounding petals ask the students to create drawings or words of people whom they like, things that they enjoy doing, and talents that they have.

Story: "Swimmy" (Grades 3–6)

Based on the book Swimmy *by Leo Lionni.*

Although an outcast in his community, Swimmy, a very special fish, ultimately becomes a hero and problem solver who teaches his peers a valuable lesson about working together and effecting change.

Once upon a time, there was a happy school of fish that lived somewhere under the vast sea. All the little fish in this family were red, except for one special fish, who was as black as a new moon sky. In addition to being a different color from the others, this little fish was able to swim much more quickly than his cousins and siblings. Swimmy was his name.

After the school of fish swam happily for a long while, they came upon a large tuna fish, who appeared to be furious and hungry. This big, scary fish came charging through the waves, making a swishing sound as he zoomed along. Then, in an instant, in one huge swallow, he consumed all of the little red fish. Swimmy was the only fish that escaped.

Lonely and frightened and extremely sad, Swimmy swam by himself into the deep abyss. As he swam deeper and farther, he noticed how beautiful his surroundings looked. He began to marvel at the creatures he was passing on his friendless journey.

In time, his loneliness was forgotten as he wondered at all the amazing things around him. First, he saw a jellyfish called a Medusa, all wiggly and glowing. Then, he came upon a lobster who, like a complex machine, was able to swirl water around herself because she had so many parts. Then he saw bunches of strange-looking lacy seaweed creatures that looked like sugar candy. Swimmy was so entranced by this seaweed that he almost got caught in the stringy forest that danced and waved around him. Just then he noticed an eel going past with a very, very, very long tail, a tail so long that you could not remember where it started or where it ended.

Suddenly, as Swimmy was passing wide-eyed among the sea anemones (who resembled pink palm trees being blown by the wind), he saw a new group of little red fish. These fish, who resembled his own school, were hiding in the crevices of the rocks. He was overjoyed and called out, hoping to get their attention.

"Hello," he said, "I'm so excited to see you. Let's play and swim together and see all the fantastic things that I have discovered!" But the little red fish tried furiously and frantically to get past him, saying that they could not play "because the massive, angry fish will follow them and gulp them down in one bite."

Swimmy was terribly disheartened to hear that the big fish had come back and he was sad to see how fear was keeping these fish from exploring their beautiful world. So, Swimmy tried to convince them that rather than live in terror, they should all work together to come up with some clever way to free them from this dread. But the school of little fish insisted that nothing could be done.

Undaunted and determined to find a solution, Swimmy thought hard about what he and the school of red fish could do to stop the big fish. He thought and thought. All of a sudden, he shouted, "I have it! I know what we can do. We can all join together so that we look like the biggest fish in the whole ocean!"

So Swimmy showed all the little red fish how to swim close together in a big fish-shape formation. And they practiced and practiced until they got it right. Then Swimmy told them he would be the eye. And so, they swam and swam and swam long and hard through the clear morning water and through the dappled midday sun, and together they chased the big fish away!

Act Out the Story

Please note: "Swimmy" workshops can be spread over three or four periods. Students probe concepts of collaboration and cooperation as they explore the ingenuity of a peacemaker who comes up with a striking idea for invoking change—an idea that necessitates group commitment and empathic collaboration to deal with a menacing bully.

These sessions include ideas for those who would like to collaborate with the art teacher to create an undersea environment in which to set the play.

Session 1: Introduction to "Swimmy"

Goal: Students explore the concepts of being excluded from and becoming part of a community.

Materials: Drum and mallet or coffee can and stick.

Warm-Up

1. Ask the students if they have ever been bullied or badgered by someone or some group.

   - "Was there a person who came to your aid, who was able to help change the situation for the better?"
   - "What did you do to help the situation?"
   - "Was there one person who became the leader, who helped the group handle the situation? If so, what happened—or did not happen?"

2. Explain to the students that for three or four periods they will be acting out a story about groups of fish in a fantastical undersea environment who solve a big problem with a bully through cooperation with others.

3. Guide students to imagine that they are a fish and are gently gliding their fish-body arms as if silently and smoothly swimming in the sea.

Development

1. Tell the story in your own words.

2. Elicit some good things that the students saw or felt in the story. Focus on the different feelings evoked.

3. Help students create a sense of underwater silence through collaborative teamwork. To begin, guide them to make steady,

uninterrupted, soft water sounds. Strike your drum or make a clapping sound to stop them abruptly. The players are to keep repeating the exercise until everyone stops at precisely the same moment. The demarcation of sound and no sound should be striking. The players have to work together to accomplish complete cooperative silence. Repeat the exercise, this time making crashing wave sounds.

4. Divide the class into two groups. Each group sits and watches as the other group does the movement. Ask one section to move in tandem into geometric shapes as you count to the drumbeat. Do the same with a second group.

- Form a circle to the count of 7.
- Form a square to the count of 10.
- Form an *S* to the count of 8.
- Form an *X* to the count of 9.
- Form a rectangle to the count of 5.

Repeat these shapes—first in silence, then

- With half of the group's eyes closed and in silence
- With half of the group's eyes closed with talking
- In slow motion

Wrap-Up

Focus on Content

Ask students what they think they learned from the experiences. Discuss who became the leaders and why. Ask such questions as

- "What happened when speech was restricted? When sight was restricted? Who helped whom?"

- "What is *body language*? What did you notice about the body language of the groups?"

- "What kinds of positive actions took place during the exercise?"

Enrichments and Extensions

- Guide students to use "hand darting" exercises that demonstrate angry or peaceful motions. Ask them to imagine that they are angry or peaceful fish darting through the ocean.

- Encourage students to describe types of fish and underwater flora and fauna that they have seen or imagined. Perhaps they have visited aquariums and have studied ocean ecology and can draw from their experience. Focus especially on fish, shellfish, underwater mammals, coral, and plants that inhabit the environment. Emphasize sensory aspects that they can think about, such as the sights, sounds, smell, and feel of water.

- Ask the class to describe in their notebooks seaweed, coral, undersea colors, and light patterns. Discuss relevant aspects of what underwater worlds may be like. What are their colors and shapes? Inform students that their notes will become the basis for a sea world environment that they will create for a play about Swimmy.

Session 2: Getting Ready to Act Out the Story

Goal: Students will review the story and determine the scenes that will make up the play.

Materials: The story and a drum and mallet or a stick and can.

Warm-Up

Review the story.

- Have the students, working in pairs (Student A and Student B), tell the story to each other.

- Coach the Student As to begin to tell the story to the Student Bs. Hit the drum at a certain point and ask them to switch so that the Student Bs pick up from the point where the Student As left off. Keep switching back and forth so that each student has a chance to be both storyteller and listener a few times around.

Development

1. Divide the class into groups each containing approximately five students, who should decide among themselves who will play different parts. Then, as leader, tell the story through simple narration so that each group can simultaneously act it out using words or pantomime.

2. Have students mutually decide on role assignments and distribution of characters.

3. Make sure that students understand that each scene has a beginning, a middle (conflict), and an end (solution).

4. Guide them to perform scenes in the classroom for peers.

Wrap-Up

1. Evaluate scenes in light of richness of exploration of concepts, character, and plot portrayal.

Focus on Content

2. Ask questions such as

- "What did you observe about the actions of Swimmy and Tuna?"
- "What do you think a peacemaker is? What do you think the characteristics of a peace seeker are? Do you think Swimmy is a peacemaker? How so?"
- "Do you think that there is a difference in the kinds of things solitary individuals can do in contrast with those things that groups working together can accomplish? Which solutions seem most effective to you—the individual or group efforts? Or a combination? Why do you think so?"

Extensions and Enrichments

- Join the small groups during rehearsals, in role as a character from the story to inspire dialogue, further the action, and help create insight for students to reflect on the story.

Session 3: Act Out the Story for Other Classes

Warm-Up

- Guide students to do the mirror game (see p. 39) but as characters in "Swimmy."

Development

- String the scenes together to make a play, preferably performed in the same space in which the group prepared, with the audience coming to that space in the room to become spectators. Use simple costume pieces and props.

Wrap-Up

Use the rubric on p. 12 to assess the enactment for discussion and revision.

Creating an Environment for Swimmy

Goal: Students will create a collaborative fantasy undersea scenic environment for a play about Swimmy.

Materials: Found objects to create an underwater sea world for the play: bubble plastic from packaging; green or brown plastic garbage bags cut into strips; lace doilies dangling from string; strips of filmy, shiny fabrics; a grid of knotted latticework made out of rope or heavy string; paper, cellophane, foil, and sparkling blue and green fabrics; buttons; sparkles; paint; paper (for making stuffed or one-dimensional fish to hang on a rope or heavy string grid); lace; mirror paper; plastic webbing from old beach chairs that can be pulled apart; strips of wool and raffia; rope, hemp, jute, and such. Make sure everything is super clean.

Warm-Up

- Share and discuss with students undersea photos and pictures, especially those that depict colorful and exotic sea creatures.

Development

1. Collect magical materials, such as those described earlier.

2. Make imaginative fish and sea foliage out of papers, such as eels, shells, coral, sea anemones, and star fish, sea horses, and fantastical fauna and flora.
   Here are examples:

3. Create webbing across the ceiling of the room. This webbing can be made out of rope, hemp, jute, or any other material tied and knotted to provide a hanging environment for your fish and sea foliage.

4. Hang fish and foliage within the webbing.

Ongoing Extensions and Enrichments

- Paint some of the fish and foliage with phosphorescent "black light paint." With the room darkened as much as possible, shine a black light (inexpensive bulb and apparatus can be bought at any lighting store that sells specialty bulbs) on the sea environment. The painted areas will glow magically in the dark.

- Intermingle the student actors and the audience within this environment.

- Guide student actors after a performance to remain in character and speak directly to the audience to discuss issues raised in the production.

Student hanging the undersea creatures for the "Swimmy" environment. (Photo: Dorothy Napp Schindel)

Template for creating undersea "Swimmy fish" to use in the "Swimmy" environment. (Illustration by Dorothy Napp Schindel)

Template for creating undersea angry fish to use in the "Swimmy" environment. (Illustration by Dorothy Napp Schindel)

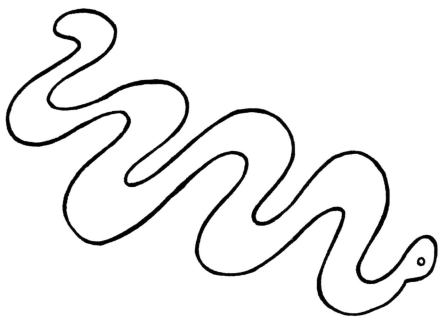

Template for creating undersea eel to use in the "Swimmy" environment. (Illustration by Dorothy Napp Schindel)

Template for creating undersea starfish to use in the "Swimmy" environment. (Illustration by Dorothy Napp Schindel)

More Helpful Tips: Creating Scenes and Assigning Roles

1. Coach students to divide the story into sequential scenarios following a story line, using the original story as the base. Each scene can have anywhere from two to six players. Guide each group to go to a different part of the room (its own personal exploration space).

2. Instruct students to flesh out scenes. For example, Scene 1 can have Swimmy and his red brothers and sisters swimming happily in the sea (through movement and sound) or perhaps playing a game of catch with a sea sponge. Remind students to give each character personality traits so that each player makes a unique contribution to the scene. The characters, for example, might include Swimmy, a cousin named Wilma, a sister named Frances, and so on. Wilma can be taunting Swimmy and asking others to do the same.

3. Encourage students to create a whole series of these scenes, making sure to follow the story line. Continue until all the scenes are assigned to groups. Remind students to make sure that each scene moves the play forward and that it encompasses a range of characters. For instance, the character of Swimmy can be in many scenes, portrayed by multiple actors. Dividing the play in this manner gives a lot of students the opportunity to play major roles, in contrast to having one student be labeled the "star."

More Examples of Possible Scenes in Sequence for Swimmy

Remember that each scene should have a beginning (conflict situation), a middle (conflict or problem developed), and an ending (resolution of conflict).

CHAPTER FOUR

Scene 1

Plot: Swimmy is swimming with his family in a corner of the sea but is treated badly by his siblings.

Characters: Swimmy, uncle, cousins.

Action: Swimmy's cousins make fun of him. His uncle insists that Swimmy stay out of the way because he swims too fast and may hurt one of his cousins. Or perhaps Swimmy bumps into one of his cousins and is accused of being clumsy. Swimmy tries to make his family like him by saying and doing kind things.

Scene 2

Plot: A school of big tuna fish come through the sea and interact with the little red fish. One of the tuna fish eats all the red fish. Swimmy swims away all alone.

Characters: Swimmy, three nice tuna fish, one mean tuna fish.

Action: The nice tuna fish want to make friends with the little red fish. They are not happy with the big mean tuna and continually have to tell him that his bullying actions are not appropriate. But the mean tuna taunts and then gobbles up the little red fish anyway, causing the other tuna fish to want nothing to do with him after the attack. The bad tuna swims away alone, vowing to be more menacing than ever.

Scene 3

Plot: As he travels through the undersea world, Swimmy comes upon many fascinating and beautiful creatures.

Characters: Lobster, seaweed, sea anemone, eel, jellyfish, and any other fantastic creatures that the students have created during prior explorations.

Action: Swimmy tries to make friends with all the beautiful creatures he passes. Some are having problems, such as trouble swimming or keeping their color intense, and they see Swimmy as an intruder. But Swimmy is persistent, helps them out, and gains their respect.

Scene 4

Plot: Swimmy meets a new school of red fish. They are afraid of being eaten by the same Big Tuna, who has been menacing them.

Characters: Swimmy, Big Tuna, frightened little Red Fish.

Action: Swimmy tries to convince them that it is silly being afraid all of the time because, as he points out, you would not be able to enjoy life and all the beautiful things there are to do and see.

Scene 5

Plot: Swimmy comes up with the idea of being the eye of one big fish, teaches the Red Fish how to swim in formation, and leads them to safety by chasing the big fish away.

Characters: Create many different characters for the Red Fish.

Action: They can all be arguing and trying to convince Swimmy that this is a futile effort. Eventually, through movement and sound patterns, they all follow him and chase the big fish away. This would be a good place for choral speaking or for the recitation of a group-created poem about working together.

More Helpful Tips: Designing a Scenario

Young people enjoy acting out stirring stories that deal with real-life persons or characters that stand up to bullies. These stories often recount acts of courage set against a social backdrop. One such story familiar to most young people concerns Rosa Parks, the Montgomery, Alabama, seamstress who in 1955 helped to dramatically change the course of the civil rights movement.

This section offers an example of how a scenario can be helpful to organize a sequence of events in a structured outline that serves as the basis for an improvised play that can be acted out or used to write an individual or group play. You have already seen how the additional scenes in "Swimmy" can offer many exciting opportunities for enactment.

A scenario is a written, scene-by-scene breakdown of what happens in the play. After the scenario is designed, dialogue—which can be improvised or written—is created right on the spot by the students, with the help of your side coaching.

The Scenario: "Rosa Parks Responds With Pride!"

This scenario was designed by students at PS 183 in Manhattan.

Scene 1: Prologue—today, a bus stop in Montgomery, Alabama. Pat Johnson, a hard-hitting newspaper reporter for the *Montgomery Times* is standing on the corner, waiting for an important person to interview about an event that took place five decades ago—right at this very spot. Pat begins to tell the story to a friendly passerby as we flashback to . . .

Scene 2: The same place, a bus stop—December 1, 1955. Rosa Parks and a Close Friend (who works with her in a department store) are waiting for the bus. The Close Friend wants Rosa to go shopping with her, but Rosa, who is tired, wants to go directly home. The Close Friend says good-bye, leaving Rosa to wait for the bus.

Scene 3: Aboard the bus. Instantly, the classroom chairs become the bus. The Bus Driver says hello to Passengers as they board the bus. Rosa takes a front seat, as a Passenger says some disapproving words. But another Passenger defends her decision to sit in the section reserved for Whites only.

Scene 4: The next stop. Calling "All aboard, all aboard," the Bus Driver and more Passengers get on board. One of them wants Rosa's seat. The Bus Driver asks Rosa to give up her seat. She refuses to move. Pat Johnson relates (as the scene is enacted) how the Bus Driver stopped the bus and tells Rosa several times to move. She refuses, each time, to do so. The Bus Driver calls the Police, and Rosa is arrested.

Scene 5: Police station, a half hour later. (Chairs are moved instantly to become the police station waiting room.) Pat Johnson relates how Rosa was escorted to the police station and detained for several hours, waiting for the Bus Driver to finish his route and come to the police station to file a complaint.

Scene 6: Holt Street Baptist Church, that evening. (The chairs now become the church, where all the players are sitting.) Pat Johnson relates (as the scene is enacted) the events of December 1, 1955, the day that Rosa was scheduled to pay her fine—and the passionate rally at the church, where it was decided that a massive boycott of Montgomery, Alabama, buses would take place. The young minister there was Dr. Martin Luther King Jr., who spoke.

DR. KING: There comes a time that people get tired. We are here this evening to say to those who have mistreated us so that we are tired. Tired of being segregated and humiliated. Tired of being kicked about by the brutal feeling of oppression. For many years we have shown amazing patience, but we can no longer be patient with anything less than freedom and justice. One of the great glories of democracy is to protest for rights!

(Cheers from the congregation.)

ALL:

(Sing)

We shall not,
We shall not be moved.
We shall not,
We shall not be moved.
Just like a tree
That's standing by the water,
We shall not be moved!

(Second chorus joined in by audience.)

Scene 7: Epilogue—today. We find out that the person Pat Johnson has been waiting for is none other than Rosa Parks herself. Pat inquires how Rosa feels about then—and now—as the play concludes.

Of course, such a scenario and enactment of the play would include pointed questions for discussion, enabling the students to flesh out the story with research and discovery during the rehearsal process. Such questions, depending on age appropriateness, might include

- "Why do you think Rosa was being picked on in the bus?"

- "Do you think the passenger, the bus driver who picked on Rosa, and the policeman who arrested her were bullies? Why or why not?"

- "How did Rosa and the Dr. Martin Luther King Jr. deal with Rosa's arrest? What do you think of the actions they took? Why do you say this?"

Scenarios can take many different shapes, such as outlines, flow charts, and step diagrams. Whatever form they do take, they are designed with the purpose of helping students get their thoughts in order and best serve the structure of the play that they will flesh out with improvisation and writing.

Helpful Resources

Beane, A. L. (1999). *The bully-free classroom*. Minneapolis, MN: Free Spirit.

Bruchac, Joseph. (1999). *Eagle song*. New York: Puffin Books. A novel about an aboriginal boy who is pushed around for being different.

Gogoll, Martine. (1994). *Rosie's story*. Noela Young (Ill.). New York: Mondo.

Kreidler, William M. (1984). *Creative conflict resolutions: More than 200 activities for keeping peace in the classroom*. Glenview, IL: Scott, Foresman.

Lionni, Leo. (1968). *Swimmy*. New York: Random House.

Rigby, Karen. (2001). *Stop the bullying: A handbook for teachers*. Markham, ON: Pembroke.

Stones, Rosemary. (1993). *Don't pick on me: How to handle bullying*. Markham, ON: Pembroke.

Wells, Rosemary. (1998). *Yoko*. New York: Little, Brown. About a young Japanese girl who brings sushi to school for lunch and is teased for being "weird."

CHAPTER FIVE
ENVISIONING PEACE

People often consider peace as an inactive or passive state. Conflict, on the other hand, is frequently viewed as being exciting and packed with action and intrigue. Wouldn't it be wonderful if we could envision peaceful actions, peaceful solutions, and peaceful endings to conflict situations that promote caring, understanding, empathy, and unbiased perceptions of others? Wouldn't it be novel to envision peace as an energizing life-changing force?

Envisioning a peaceful future and remembering when we felt peaceful are activities that everyone can do and everyone can share. Peace is not just the absence of war and conflict but rather an active challenging state in which justice prevails. If students engage in brainstorming about the significance of peace, perhaps they can generate powerful images that will inspire them—images of people who help one another, share resources, and resolve conflicts effectively.

In this section students explore, among other resources, part of a poem by Langston Hughes, and they place themselves inside the world of the *Peaceable Kingdom*, by the artist Edward Hicks. They will play Dr. Martin Luther King Jr., calling for the struggle for equality and rights at a famous human rights march. Such works encourage racial harmony and hold up a vision of what is possible.

Students have an opportunity to dramatize poems and stories about working for peace, ranging from enacting the heroic struggle of an eleven-year-old Japanese girl named Sadako to playing powerful generals and modest ducks in contention for a peaceful world. They will play a wise Hermit who helps a concerned woman to help her husband who has returned wearily from war. They will enact a delightful Native American dance poem about a peacemaker's hopes to unify tribes who have for too long fought each other. They will imagine a world where greed, selfishness, misunderstanding, and intolerance have no place, a place where people can live and work in harmony.

If we dare to dream, perhaps such visions can move us into a new era in which senseless violence becomes a thing of the past and fair-mindedness propels us forward. As the wise proverb has it, an institution is often the length of a person's shadow. Ultimately, it is our hope that students will come to recognize they can personally effect peace and bring about change in feelings and behaviors through everyday simple actions.

Story: "The Tree of Peace"—Native American Story (Grades 3–6)

Can warring nations learn to live in harmony with the help of a peacemaker?

(Peace Seekers from the Five Nations enter the playing space and face Peacemaker.)

PEACEMAKER: After a long and bloody war between the five nations, I see that some of you still carry weapons that may be used not just for hunting but for fighting ... though you promised there would be no more fighting between the nations. *(Some of the assembled are holding, in pantomime, knives and bows and arrows. The Peace Seekers listen intently.)*

PEACEMAKER: Now I ask you to uproot the tree standing here, and I challenge you to bury weapons of war beneath it so that they will be carried away forever by strong currents underneath the ground. *(One by one, the Peace Seekers from the Five Nations cast their weapons of war into the hole left by the uprooting of the tree.)*

PEACE SEEKER #1: We will also bury our feelings of ...

PEACE SEEKER #2: Hatred ...

PEACE SEEKER #3: Greed ...

PEACE SEEKER #4: Jealousy . . .

PEACE SEEKER #5: Yes . . . bury all of these . . . all . . . in the ground. *(This is shown through movement and pantomime. Peacemaker approaches the Peace Seekers.)*

PEACEMAKER: Good. Now let us replant the tree on top of the weapons mixed with the feelings of hatred. *(This they all do in pantomime.)*

PEACE SEEKER #1: From the base of the tree will come four white roots facing north, south, east, and west. *(Gently waves a white scarf in one direction.)*

PEACE SEEKER #2: *(Gently waves the second scarf in a different direction.)* Many nations will come and recognize the tree's purpose . . .

PEACE SEEKER #3: *(Gently waves the third scarf in a different direction.)* Many individuals will see the roots and take shelter . . .

PEACE SEEKER #4: *(Waves the last scarf in still another direction.)* . . . Underneath this tree as symbol of the future.

PEACEMAKER: *(The Peace Seekers stand in a circle around the tree of peace. The Peacemaker brings forth a single arrow.)* This will be called the Tree of Peace, and its greenery will represent the peace you have made. See this arrow that can be used for hunting. When you are one nation, like this lone arrow, we are nearly broken. *(Brings forth five arrows bound together.)* But when we are bound together five as one, as this bundle, we stand as a symbol of unity and strength.

(All the Peace Seekers hold hands in a circle.)

PEACEMAKER: Some will come and try to hack at the roots and will not understand us. In this case, the tree will weaken . . . we will be burdened with heaviness. If the Peace Tree begins to fall, it must land on our joined hands . . . never let its leaves touch the ground . . . help carry the weight of the tree . . . lend a hand . . . raise the Tree of Peace again.

(The story-mime concludes with a ceremonial movement/dance.)

Act Out the Story

Recommendation: This story-mime is designed for two or three sessions.

Goal: Students will enact through pantomime and dance a Native American myth.

Materials: Copies of the story.

Warm-Up

Create and practice the ceremonial movement/dance "Tree of Peace," which concludes the play. The class can make up the words to the dance based on research or the content of the story.

Development

Focus on Content

1. Tell the story. Have the students retell the story in their own words.

2. Ask, "Who is the Peacemaker? What does she or he look like in the story? What does he or she want? What feelings does the Peacemaker evoke?"

---

3. Lay out where the action will take place. Decide if the Tree of Peace will be pantomimed or made from paper.

4. Choose the cast. Students can double up on roles.

5. Break down the play into several scenes.

6. Run through the presentation several times.

7. Invite a class to come see the show.

Wrap-Up

Discuss the story. Ask, "What worked? Why? What didn't work as well? Why? Why do you think the story was appealing?" Encourage students to give examples, showing how the story had special meaning for them.

Creating the environment for the Five Nations folktale "The Tree of Peace." (Photo: Robert Iulo)

Extensions and Enrichments

Encourage students to find additional Native American stories dealing with peace to read, enact, and reflect on.

How to Make a Shadow Play

Because you are dealing with shadows, search for material containing elements of mystery and fantasy. The students can also experiment with magical shadow effects, such as creating the illusion of growing, shrinking, double images, and flying (which the cranes do in the story "Sadako and the Thousand Cranes").

Shadow Screen

1. Use either a white cotton bed sheet or a white window shade. It is essential that the material be see-through or translucent, taut, wrinkle-free—and clean.

2. Stretch the material over a frame or hang it tautly between two posts. Any wrinkles will distort the shadows made with puppets or by the human body. A five-by-eight-foot screen is a good size to work with.

3. Mask, if possible, all sides of the frame to conceal the bodies of the operators.

Light Source

1. Use a 150–200 watt lightbulb placed approximately six feet behind the white sheet or screen used.

2. Make sure that the lightbulb is placed high enough to eliminate the light operator's shadow.

3. Help students experiment with using a tensor light, flashlight, or other sources of light. Shining two lights on the screen at the same time will produce amazing double-shadow effects.

Shadow Puppets

1. Guide students to design and draw their shadow puppets.

2. Help younger students cut their puppet figures out of black construction paper or cardstock.

3. Guide students to create fascinating color effects—for example, in the Sadako story, the lantern can light up by pasting colored cellophane or candy wrappers over slits in the figures. If needed, holes can be perforated with a small hole puncher.

4. Use rulers or dowel sticks attached to the puppets with scotch tape that students will manipulate on the shadow screen. Any rod used should be long enough to allow the operator to stand behind the light source (otherwise, bodies will show up). Coach students to gently press the shadow puppets against the screen. Instant shadow magic guaranteed!

Shadow Scenery

1. Guide students to limit their scenery to one or two side pieces framing the center acting area.

2. Have them pin black construction paper or black cardstock right onto the screen.

3. Guide students to cut out sections of the construction paper for great colored effects. They can also place translucent colored material over the openings.

Shadow Costumes

1. Help students use simple but imaginative touches to dress their shadow figures. For example, twisted straw or frayed string can suggest different kinds of hair.

2. Make sure students understand that the effect their puppets create in shadow is the key element in this type of play. They

should not judge their final results by what appears in daylight but as shadows.

Shadow Poem: "Sadako and the Thousand Cranes" (Grades 3–6)

An 11-year-old girl in her death leaves a legacy of peace.

> The family of 11-year-old Sadako Sasaki,
> Her mother, father, sister, and two brothers
> Observed Peace Day to remember the day
> When a terrible bomb was dropped on Japan,
> Killing Sadako's grandmother and thousands of others.
> That happened on August 6, 1945. Sadako was two.
> *(Place golden frame of Grandmother Obo on screen.)*
> Obo Chan was her grandmother's name.
> The family had a lovely picture of her
> Set in a beautiful golden frame.
> *(Place figures of six lanterns on screen.)*
> On Peace Day, every August sixth,
> The family lit six lanterns for their relatives
> Who had died nine years before.
> Their prayer for the future—was peace in everyone's lives.
> *(Place figure of weakened Sadako on screen.)*
> One day Sadako felt unsteady and so weak
> She was sent to a hospital to be treated for leukemia
> Caused by the A-bomb dropped on Japan.
> With Sadako sick, everything looked very bleak.
> *(Place figure of Chizuko on screen.)*
> Her friend Chizuko told Sadako about a story that says
> She would be granted her wish of good health . . .
> If she folded a thousand cranes.
> *(Place figures of several cranes on screen.)*
> Sadako began working to make 1,000 paper cranes.
> Friends and family visited her in the hospital.
> She still had hope even though she was in great pain.
> One day, when she had a very weak feeling
> She made . . . her last one . . . her 644th crane . . .
> *(Place figures of golden paper cranes on screen.)*

Sadako saw the other cranes hanging from the ceiling.
Smiling, she took her last breath, family at her side.
October 25 is the sad day she died.
Her classmates folded 366 more golden cranes
To be buried with her, yes, a total of a thousand.
So we can say Sadako did get her wish.
People will remember her in their hearts forever
(Place figure of Sadako on screen.)
People today still place paper peace cranes
On Sadako's statue in Peace Park
On August 6, Peace Day.
And on the base of the statue we see
What all of us would like to say:
This is our cry.
This is our prayer.
Peace in the world.
(Place figure of Sadako watching paper cranes flying on screen.)

Create a Shadow Play From a Story-Poem

Goal: Students will make a shadow play from the story-poem "Sadako and the Thousand Cranes," based on the book by Eleanor Coerr.

Materials: The story-poem "Sadako and the Thousand Cranes," puppets, screen, light source, construction paper, blunt scissors, long sticks or rulers.

Warm-Up

Guide students to cut out pictures of doves from black construction paper, attach them to long sticks or rulers, and press against a shadow screen with a light behind the screen. Pull down window shades and turn off all classroom lights. Move the crane shadow puppets to fly across around the screen. Turn on lights. Conduct a discussion of what peace means to the students. Ask why the dove is considered a symbol of peace.

Development

1. Ask students, "Has there ever been a time when a friend gave you a special gift? How did you feel about getting it?"

2. Provide the necessary background on World War II—who was at war and why. Focus discussion on the last days of the war.

3. Explain or elicit from students how World War II ended in 1945—by America dropping the atomic bomb on two cities in Japan. Ask them, "Do you think there are times when a country must go to war? If so, under what circumstances?"

Focus on Content

4. Discuss with class the major feelings that people have regarding the pros and cons—for and against—of dropping the bomb (e.g., for: saved the lives of millions of American soldiers who would have died had the war continued; against: needless killing of thousands of innocent Japanese civilians).

5. Guide the class to read the story-poem individually and together. Point out that it was written by us based on the book *Sadako and the Thousand Cranes* by Eleanor Coerr.

6. Ask such questions as

   - "Do you believe that it was right for the atomic bomb to be dropped on Hiroshima? Why or why not?"
   - "What was Sadako's wish? Why do you think she wanted to fold a thousand cranes?"
   - "How did Sadako's classmates keep her memory alive?"
   - "Do you agree or disagree that Sadako got her wish? Why do you think so?"

---

7. Prepare students to make a shadow play based on the poem. See instructions for making a shadow play (pp. 130–132).

8. Guide students to create the shadow figures of the paper cranes that several of Sadako's friends gave her.

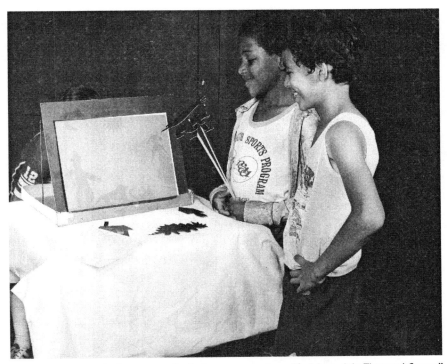

Making and showing shadow puppets for the Japanese story-poem "Sadako and the Thousand Cranes."
(Photo: Milton Polsky)

9. Direct students to slowly move the shadow puppets on the screen as different narrators read the story-poem aloud.

10. Present the shadow play to other classes. Get some feedback on how it went. Redo any aspects of the shadow play that are not clear and present the play again.

Wrap-Up

Ask students again, "How did Sadako's classmates keep her memory alive? How did you keep her memory alive?"

Extensions and Enrichments

Consider having the class act out some other stories, such as "Bring Back a Tiger's Whisker," which follows.

135

Story: "Bring Back a Tiger's Whisker"—Korean Folktale (Grades 3–6)

Can a person help bring peace of mind to someone he or she does not know?

Yun Ok needed the help of a Hermit who lived in a hut in the mountains of Korea.

"Why do you come to visit me?" the wise man asked when the young woman entered his hut.

"I need one of your famous magic potions to cure my stress!" she said.

"What is bothering you, Yun Ok?"

"My husband, who has retired from the wars after three years, seems so lost. He rarely speaks to anyone, including me, his wife. He doesn't listen to anyone. He leaves the room in anger if the food I prepare for him displeases him. He just sits on top of the hill near our home. Instead of working in the field, he just looks out at the sea . . . so lost."

The Hermit answered, "I am so sorry. This seems to happen often to young men returning from the wars."

"That is what is bothering him—and me, for I love him so. I need a potion, oh Wise One, for him so that he can return to his former gentle and loving self."

"It's not so simple to prepare such a potion. Return in a week, and I will let you know what is needed for a the potion that will help you help him."

Yun Ok returned in a week, and the wise Hermit said, "Yes, I can provide the potion, but what will be needed to make it work is the whisker of a live tiger."

"That is too hard," Yun Ok said. "How can I possibly bring a fierce tiger's whisker back to you?"

"If that is what you need to help your husband, you shall do it," and then the Hermit said no more.

Yun Ok went back to her home and thought about what she had to do. She waited until her husband slept, and she crept away from her house with a bowl of rice and meat in her hand to the mountain cave where the tiger lived.

She stayed at a distance from the cave, but the tiger did not come out when she called him to come out. For the next three nights she went closer and closer to the tiger's cave. The tiger got used to her coming to him. Finally, on the third night, she was so close to the tiger that she could talk to him in a small voice. The next night, she looked straight into the tiger's eyes.

After several months of visits, the tiger felt so comfortable eating her food that she was able to pet him and talk soothingly to him. "I need to have one of your whiskers. Please let me have one and please do not show your anger."

The tiger nodded that it was alright to do so. She was careful to cut one of his whiskers. The tiger was not angry at all. Yun Ok thanked the tiger and, tightly holding the whisker, went down the trail to the Hermit's hut. She handed the whisker to the Hermit. She asked him, "Now can you prepare the potion to cure my husband of his sadness?" Strangely to her, he dropped the whisker into his fireplace.

"Oh," Yun Ok cried out, "you just spoiled it—everything just went up in smoke. It took months for me to get that whisker. I had to, very slowly, gain the tiger's trust. I talked gently with him. I was so patient. Night after night I came with food. Even though the tiger did not eat, I never gave up. I rubbed its head, and it made contented sounds. I won that tiger over with understanding and kindness."

"That was good," said the Hermit, smiling.

"But look what you did," she said. "You threw the whisker I brought you—as you requested—into the fire."

The Hermit smiled again and said, "If you can do that with a wild animal and get—with patience and understanding—its confidence, imagine what will you be able to do with your husband, with patience, understanding, and love. Go to him now. You are ready, and with patience, understanding, and love, so too will he be ready."

Yun Ok understood. She thanked the Hermit and went down the trail to be with her husband.

Act Out the Story in Shadow

Goal: Students will discuss how people can help each other to achieve a peaceful state of mind, and they will act out a story using shadow puppets.

Materials: Copies of the story "Bring Back a Tiger's Whisker" and shadow theater materials: a translucent white sheet, black construction paper, blunt scissors, tensor light.

Warm-Up

Focus on Content

1. Discuss the story. Ask, "Do you think the Hermit was able to help Yun Ok? Why or why not? Do you think he was able to help her husband? Why or why not? Do you think people are able to help people they do not even know to have a peaceful state of mind? Discuss your feelings about the subject."

---

2. Have students, in place, stretch out and silently make the figure of a tiger. Have them quickly return to their own body shapes and then back to the tiger's shape several times. Coach them, in pairs, to discuss or act out a brief scene with Yun Ok and her husband, showing him under a great deal of stress.

Development

1. Guide students to structure the scenes in the story and the characters in them. For example, will there be a scene with Yun Ok and her husband? Students can make a scenario for their shadow theater show.

2. Coach them to make the shadow puppets from black construction paper. They can also make from black construction paper shadow scenery, such as Korean mountains, rivers, the sun, the Hermit's hut, and so on. Help students put the dowel stick on their puppets. Review the procedures for making a shadow theater play (see pp. 130–132).

3. Direct students to follow their scenarios and act out the story in shadow with a tensor light placed behind the shadow screen.

4. Discuss how the shadow play can be improved, and rework scenes that need to be made clearer.

5. Invite a class to see a polished performance.

Wrap-Up

1. Assess with students how the rehearsal and production process went. Were the shadows clear? Were the actions of the characters clear and interesting? Is there anything the students want to add, change, or delete?

2. Discuss if the story's theme of helping and becoming a peacemaker for someone seeking help was clear, interesting, and thoughtful.

Extensions and Enrichments

- Suggest that students draw some of the scenes they enacted.

Story: "The Duck in the Gun"—New Zealand (Grades 3–6)

A mother duck, through steadfast tenacity, bravery, and determination, succeeds in changing attitudes, protecting human rights, and preventing the annihilation of two villages.

This lesson consists of two sessions.

Note: "The Duck in the Gun" is adapted from the book of the same title written by Joy Cowley, one of New Zealand's most prominent and respected authors. Because of its powerful antiwar message, the book gained a following across the globe. It is one of ten children's books selected for the Hiroshima Peace Museum.

Once there were two villages. Each village had a general and an army. One of the generals decided that he wanted to start a war with the other village. This way, he thought, he could take over that village and expand his land. He would be ruler of all the people in both villages. So, he pointed his large cannon in the direction of the other village and asked his Chief Gunner to get ready to shoot. The Chief Gunner came up to the General and said that he could not possibly fire the gun.

"Well, why not?" implored the angry General.

"Well," said the Chief Gunner, "we can't load the gun, sir."

"What do you mean you can't load the gun? Of course, you can load the gun. It is in perfect working condition."

"No, sir, I can't load the gun because there is a duck in it! A duck has made a nest in our gun, sir."

"You mean a duck is sitting in our gun and won't come out?"

"Yes, it has made a nest in there, sir," said the Chief Gunner. "In fact, I put my hand in to get it, but I can't reach it, sir."

The General looked deep inside the gun and saw two big, beautiful duck eyes staring back at him. He tried to coax Duck to come out. He sweetly called to her, "Here ducky, ducky."

But Duck quacked repeatedly and refused to move. By this time, the General was getting very angry and pounded on the gun. "You come out of there this instant," he shouted at the Duck.

But nothing happened, so the General got an idea. "We can put pieces of bread at the end of the cannon, and Duck will come to get the food."

So they tried that, but it didn't work. Duck still refused to budge. The General was outraged. "How can a duck upset my plans?" he shouted.

"Sir, I have another idea," cried the Gunner. "You can fire the gun with the duck inside." The General seemed to soften and said, "Absolutely not, we will think of another idea." And he thought and thought and thought. "Aha, I've got it," he said. "We will borrow a different cannon and shoot that one!"

So the General got all dressed up in his finest uniform, donned all his many medals, took a white flag with him, and went to visit the other village to ask permission to borrow that town's cannon. But the Prime Minister of the village refused his request, saying that she couldn't possibly lend him its gun. But she suggested a plan. "We could wait three weeks until the ducklings are born and the gun is vacated."

"Let's put the war off for three weeks," the Prime Minister declared. So, the General shook hands with the Prime Minister, and they decided to hold off on the war for at least three more weeks. The General's men were very pleased because it meant that they could take a holiday and could also feed the duck whenever they pleased (when the General wasn't looking, ofcourse).

After a week, the General went back to visit the Prime Minister again. This time he asked if he could borrow money to pay his men, who—because they had no work to do—were idling about and demanding pay.

"Well, wait," said the Prime Minister. "I can't give you money to pay men who are not doing anything, but I would be happy to hire your men to paint our village. Our buildings are looking run-down, the shops are looking scruffy, and the paint on many houses is peeling. Your men could accomplish a great deal of painting over the next two weeks."

"A terrific idea," cried the General. "I will hurry and tell my men." The men were very pleased that they could make money while waiting for Duck to hatch her eggs. So they donned old clothes, picked up brushes, mixed paint, and began to restore the town. The General bided his time by lying in the sun, reading his books, and relaxing (and sneaking cake to Duck when no one was looking).

One day, the General looked through his glasses and noticed the beautiful colors the houses were being painted. So, he visited the Prime Minister and had tea with her family. When he left, he took some of the tea cakes back to Duck.

At the end of the third week, the General heard happy quacking and a whole bunch of *peep, peep, peeps*. He rang the bell as hard as he could, and his men put down their paintbrushes and came running back to hear the news.

"Look what has happened," the General said. "Duck's eggs have hatched." And one by one, the little ducklings popped their heads out of the gun. The General picked each one up carefully, until there were eight of them waddling about his feet. Then Mother Duck came along, looked up at the men and quacked very loudly. She flew down next to her babies and marched them off across the grassy hill. The men all cheered, threw their hats in the air, and yelled, "Yeah, Yeah, Yeah! Now, at last, we can have the war!"

But, quite suddenly, the men stopped cheering. "Wait a minute. We can't blow up the houses that we just painted," they said. "We will spoil the paint job. And besides, we don't want to hurt the people who live in the houses. We are very fond of them. Why would we want to have a war?"

The Chief Gunner asked the General if he could postpone the war forever so that they could finish painting the houses and then go home. "That is a very good idea," General agreed. And so, the idea of having a war was dismissed. In fact, the General became the Prime Minister's best friend. And Duck and her ducklings marched behind the military marching band when they played at his wedding to the Prime Minister's daughter!

Peace is a very good thing, indeed, they all agreed. And the ducks all quacked in agreement.

Act Out the Story

Session 1

Goal: Students will listen to and reflect on a story dealing with peacefully resolving a major conflict.

Materials: The story.

Warm-Up

1. Ask these kinds of questions:

   - "Was there a time when someone you didn't like became your friend? What happened? How did you feel about what happened?"
   - "What made you change your mind about that person?"
   - "Have you ever met anyone who you thought would be different than he or she turned out to be, once you got to know that person? Explain."

2. Explain that today students will listen to a story in which the main characters learn to change their decisions in response to an explosive situation.

3. Guide them to play "Peaceful Actions." Working in pairs, one will be a person who needs help (e.g., falling on an elbow). The other will help (e.g., putting bandage on the elbow).

Development

1. Tell the story. Try changing the dynamics of your voice— loud/soft, high/low, fast/slow. Experiment with taking on different voices for each of the characters. You might want to repeat the story, this time assigning lines to individual students

to read or improvise when you point to them during the action. Have fun with the story. Although the narrative has a serious message, the story is filled with comical, endearing overtones and ironic twists.

2. Guide students to play "Pass the Egg / Pass the Fluffy Duck."

- Coach students to stand in a circle and carefully pantomime passing an egg from person to person. Make sure they do not drop or squeeze the egg. Coach, "Keep it moving. Handle the egg very carefully. Everyone is responsible for its safety."
- Tap a student on the shoulder at some point. Ask him or her to pantomime holding on to a new fluffy duck as it hatches from the egg.
- Invite students to repeat the exercise, passing the newly born fluffy duck from person to person. Remind them once again that the group is responsible for the well-being of the duck as it is passed around the circle in pantomime.

Focus on Content

3. Guide students, working in pairs, to try on some roles:

- Coach, "Can you think of a number of different reasons why the soldiers did not want to attack the town they had just painted? Have a conversation between two soldiers as they discuss this subject. Make sure you express their feelings."
- Ask, "If Duck had decided to talk to the General, what do you think she would have said to him?" Coach students to have a discussion between Duck and the General.
- Ask, "Was there a time when someone you didn't like became your friend? What made you change your mind about that person?"
- Coach students to take on the roles of Duck and General and have a conversation. Make sure the students express their characters' feelings.

Wrap-Up

Engage the students in a lively discussion by asking these kinds of questions:

- "Do you think there was ever any reason for the General to start a war? Please explain."

- "Do you think the Prime Minister or the General was a 'peace-maker'?" Please explain.

- "Does it bother you when someone wants to hurt someone else, either physically or by saying something that is demeaning?" Please explain.

Extensions and Enrichments

After they try on various roles, guide students to write out some of the dialogue between the characters.

Session 2

Goal: Students will learn through observation and reflection how to handle potentially explosive situations.

Materials: Drum and mallet (optional).

Warm-Up

1. Direct students to take comfortable places around the classroom. Ask them to move their arms, legs, and head, high, low, and all around, as they hear the drumbeat. Instruct them, on the clap of your hands, to make a fantastic shape. Then ask them to "freeze"

- as a duck, then as a duck sitting on eggs in a gun;
- as a general, then as a general giving orders to his men;
- as one soldier, then as several soldiers painting the houses.

2. Encourage them to suggest other freeze possibilities.

Development

1. Conduct, before creating silent tableaus, a discussion with students. Ask,

   - "What are some of the things in your classroom or communities that make you so angry that you wish you could step in and do something to change the situation?" Some examples: Some classmates mess up your desk and scribble on it. A classmate picks on another because of the color of his or her hair. Your neighbor wants to start a fight to get even about something that he or she perceives as wrong.

2. Guide students to create a tableau (see pp. 18–20).

   - Coach students to show the moment in time when one of these situations happened with characters who might have been there at the time.

Focus on Content

3. Freeze the groups one at a time in their tableau. Ask these kinds of questions for each frozen scene:

   - "If you could give this pose a title, what would it be?"
   - "What are these characters thinking? How do they feel? What are these two characters saying to one another?"
   - "If this person could speak, what would he or she be feeling and saying?"

4. Guide students to create a second tableau, one that shows what the characters did to find a solution to the problem. Examples:

   - You ask the teacher for help. What would the teacher say or do?
   - You ask why the person or persons did what they did.

Wrap-Up

1. Ask,

   - "In your tableau, who became the peace seekers and why?"
   - "What are some things that can happen to people when they try to resolve conflicts or problems?"
   - "Have any one of you ever tried to resolve conflicts or problems between people? Could you share with the class the circumstances and what happened?"

2. Discuss the characters and situations created by each of the groups.

Extensions and Enrichments

- Invite the students to turn the "Duck in the Gun" story into a radio play (see pp. 82–83) or shadow play (see pp. 130–132).

- Create an environment for acting out the play for invited audiences.

- Create a town by painting buildings and houses on Kraft paper that can be attached to a wall or build Foamcore stand-up buildings. *Idea:* If you are painting on large pieces of paper, you can begin with a black-and-white town and then paint the colors on during the play.

- Create a grid system out of rope. Out of paper and other found materials, create images from the story. Hang these images from the grid. For example, guide the students to create ducks, cannons, soldier hats, paintbrushes with different colors on them, cans of paint, pieces of bread, nests, baby ducklings, faces of the soldiers, the Prime Minister, and the General. Make soldier hats out of rolled pieces of oaktag. Add peaks that have been cut out and attached. Paint designs on the hats. Use feathers, gold buttons, and sparkles to dress up the hats.

Inspiration from a painting The Peaceable Kingdom *(circa 1834), by Edward Hicks (1780–1849), from the collection of the National Gallery of Art, Washington, DC.*

Paintings and Pictures as Stimuli for Creative Drama: *The Peaceable Kingdom* by Edward Hicks (Grades 3–6)

Paintings and other works of art can be powerful catalysts for understanding concepts of peace and conflict resolution. The stylized placement of the many different animals in Edward Hicks's paintings of *The Peaceable Kingdom* suggests that under the right circumstances even those who are usually enemies can learn to set their differences aside and coexist amicably.

Background of the Artist

Edward Hicks (1780–1849), a self-taught "folk artist," was originally employed as a farmer, a sign painter, and a decorator of carriages.

A religious preacher, he was heavily influenced by passages in the Bible. He eventually developed great technical ability as a painter and became well known for his series of animal paintings entitled *The Peaceable Kingdom* (up to 100 different versions were painted by him). As a staunch Quaker and pacifist, Hicks refused to paint portraits (a popular genre at the time), which he considered too ego centered. But he did have an interest in animals and their relationships to humans in symbolic terms. Using the tradition that gives human personalities and humanistic qualities to animals, he painted many animals, juxtaposing them in unlikely pairings, to help viewers envision peaceful coexistence.

Exploring the Painting Through Movement, Sound, and Role-Play

Paintings are composed of lines, colors, and shapes. Used in subtle ways by the artist, these elements of the visual arts convey emotion and elicit visceral response to an idea or concept. For example, a harmonious picture will often have flowing or rounded lines. A curvy-lined painting or sculpture can denote confusion or uncertainty. A picture filled with conflict and emotional strife will often have jagged or zigzag lines, and a picture portraying stillness and status quo may contain straight lines at its core.

Color choices are generally more obvious. Yellow, for example, is often recognized as a happy color, but it can also represent jaundice and sickness. Transforming the attributes of lines and colors to animals and humans can help students to explore personalities and motivations for behavior.

Paintings can also help students visualize, inspire, and validate role-playing enactments. For example, the wolf and the sheep in the painting have both found the same comfortable place to take a nap. Their space is located at the foot of a big shady tree with a comfy pile of leaves at its base. But there is only room for one of them to lean up against the tree in the shade. How will they work out their problem? In a similar vein, how can this situation be applied to students' real-life situations involving space and possible conflict issues?

Act Out the Picture

Session I

Goal: Students will experience the difference between peaceful and nonpeaceful environments and discover ways to initiate change for the better.

Materials: Drum and mallet, slide (for projection) or photocopies of one of Hicks's renditions of *The Peaceable Kingdom*.

Warm-Up

1. Share with the students the information about the artist.

2. Show a copy of the painting to the class, or project a slide of it on the wall. Ask, "What do you see in the picture? What do you think each animal and person seems to be doing and feeling? Do you think the characters are behaving the way we would expect them to? Please explain." Ask, "What does a straight line mean to you?" (e.g., boring, dead, calm, determined, obsessed).

3. On your drumbeat or clap of hands, guide students to move as a straight line. Coach, "Please use the whole space and do not bump into one another. Freeze. Relax and move again. Now add a straight-line sound. Freeze, relax again." Ask, "What can you say about a curvy line?" (e.g., uncertainty, happy, not trustworthy, forgetful, confused). On your drumbeat or clap of hands, guide students to move around the room as a curvy line. Coach, "Make curvy-line sounds. Freeze in a curvy pose. Add curvy-line words. Move in slow motion."

Also ask the class to do the same for jagged or zigzag lines. Note that a drumbeat or clap of hands can suggest jagged movements.

Focus on Content

Development

1. Divide the class into pairs. Ask the partners to create an improvisational scene between a "straight line" animal and a "jagged or curvy line" animal (or between an animal and a human with those characteristics). Discuss the fact that lines can be depicted either in physical or in psychological terms or both. For example, a person can be both very stiff (physical) and obsessed with one single-minded thought (psychological). Encourage the students to be larger than life in their portrayals but true to the essence of the characters.

149

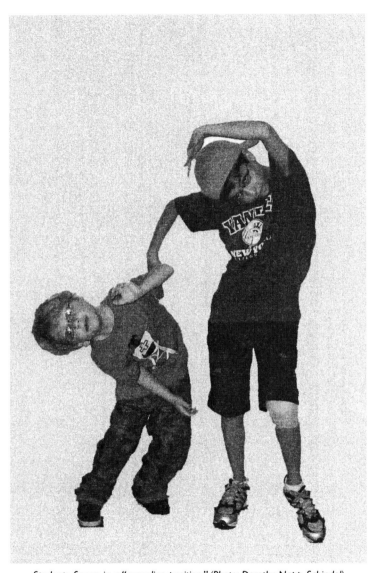

Students freeze in a "curvy-line position." (Photo: Dorothy Napp Schindel)

2. Place the scene in a shoe store setting. One of the animals or humans is the shoe salesperson; the other is buying a pair of shoes. Remind students that the scene should have a beginning (conflict situation), a middle (complication), and an end (solution). Help students establish the characters, the plot, and the setting for each scene. Work with the groups through side coaching and by taking on a character yourself. Guide students to rehearse their scenes and play them for the class.

   - Ask the observing group members after each scene to describe what they have seen. How would they classify the characters? Who was a straight-line character, who was curvy, and so on? What else did they observe? What feelings were evoked?

Wrap-Up

1. Guide the students to review the painting and respond to these kinds of questions:

   - "What kind of lines does Hicks use in this painting? What kinds of feelings are evoked?"
   - "What do these lines say about the animals and the people he is portraying?"

2. Ask, "What if the lines in the painting were changed? What would happen to the relationships in the picture?"

Extensions and Enrichments

1. Suggest that students experiment with drawing various pictures —an angry-line picture, a happy-line picture, a conglomerate-line (a line made up of both happy and angry segments) picture. They can make up a story about the angry line, the happy line, or the conglomerate line.

2. Repeat the exercise, only this time ask the students to cut out an angry shape and a happy shape from pieces of paper or cardboard and to use them as hand puppets.

Session 2

Goal: Students will visualize peaceful environments and practice ways to negotiate differences of opinions.

Materials: Drum and mallet, slide (for projection) or photocopies of Hicks's renditions of *The Peaceable Kingdom.*

Warm-Up

1. Review briefly the previous session. Ask, for example, if anyone remembers what kind of lines they saw in the Hicks painting? Ask the whole group, to a drumbeat or clap of hands, to sit as straight-line animals, then as curvy animals, then as jagged animals. Encourage them to make what they imagine are the sounds of these animals.

2. Explain to the class that they will now explore the colors in *The Peaceable Kingdom.*

   - Ask, "Why do you think Hicks used the colors he did?"

Development

1. Guide students to play "Four Corner Run-In."

   - Choose four participants to form a boxing-ring configuration. Upon hearing a color or phrase, each participant runs into the center of the ring and join others to make a group shape that responds to your suggestions.

   - Remind the participants to take different levels and stay close to one another when they make their group shape.

   - Ask the group to
     Run, run, run and take a shape as the color red.
     Move as the color red.
     Make a sound as the color red.
     Freeze. Relax.

- Choose another group to

  Run in as oozing red ketchup.

  Make a group shape as oozing red ketchup.

  Make the sound of oozing red ketchup.

  Move in slow motion as oozing red ketchup.

  Freeze. Relax.

  Run in as sour yellow lemons.

  Take a group shape as sour yellow lemons.

  Move in slow motion as sour yellow lemons.

  Say sour yellow lemon words.

  Freeze. Relax.

- Ask the class to make up its own color phrases to explore (e.g., *yucky yellow chicken fat, endless blue skies, red sky in the morning, fire and ice*).

2. Guide students to play "Colors in Conflict."
   - Ask, "What colors do you see in the Hicks painting? Why do you think the artist used these colors?"
   - Divide the class into pairs. Coach students to play scenes between the following inanimate objects: a red blotch of ketchup on a stiff white shirt and a fancy gold necklace on a grungy, old, blue T-shirt. Play the scenes again, this time finding a solution to the problems.
   - Encourage students to make up their own "colors in conflict" and play scenes between them.

Focus on Content

Wrap-Up

   Ask, "How did the characters in your scenes find ways to cooperate and come to an agreement?"

Extensions and Enrichments

Encourage students, using colored markers, to make blotches of colors that look harmonious and to draw blotches of colors that might look uncomfortable and angry with one another. Invite them to discuss the resulting differences.

Session 3

Goal: Students will relate the Hicks's painting to real-life situations.

Materials: Drum and mallet, slide (for projection) or photocopies of Hicks's renditions of *The Peaceable Kingdom.*

Warm-Up

Guide students to sit as a straight-line, curvy-line, or jagged-line animal.

Development

Focus on Content

Invite students to look at the painting again. Ask, "Do any of the animals look uncomfortable, as if they are surprised at their behavior? Why do you think this is so?"

Frozen Moment A. Conduct a discussion about the animals in the painting and what they seem to be feeling and saying to one another. Do they seem to be communicating with the humans in any way? Based on student responses, guide players, in groups, to create "frozen freeze frames or tableaus" (see pp. 18–20) to indicate what they believe the artist intended to make known through the painting.

- Ask each group to freeze tableaus while the others in the class guess what is happening in the frozen pose.

Questions to ask about the pose might include

- "What do you think the various animals and people are thinking and feeling?"

- "If these two animals could talk to each other, what do you think they would be saying?"

- "How would you title the frozen pose?"

- "If you could change the animals into people, what kind of people would they be? What would they want? Who would get in their way?" Perhaps act out a little scene between the people.

Focus on Content

Frozen Moment B. Try out this exercise.

1. Coach the students to decide on a conflict that a group of humans or animals in the picture might be experiencing. Ask the class to come up with ideas based on everyday encounters with siblings, friends, other children, and parents.

   Example: You and your sister or brother love to take a nap or read on the living room couch because it is so soft and cozy. As soon as you arrive home from school, you both rush toward the couch. But only one of you can claim that spot at that time. How would you work out the problem?

2. Guide the class to split into groups and to
   - Freeze the moment of the conflict. Ask, "Who do you think would be in the picture? What would they be doing?" Freeze the moment when they have worked out their differences.

Wrap-Up

Ask the class what they saw in these frozen tableaus. Could the problems have been worked out differently? Did any of these frozen moments remind them of their own families or friends?

Extensions and Enrichments

- Discuss, "What if this painting were a 'modern day' peaceable kingdom? Who do you think would be in the picture? What would they be doing?"

"We Still Have a Dream":
The Rev. Dr. Martin Luther King Jr.

Dramatization by Milton Polsky.

The Set

Feel free to experiment with your own simple set. For example, one class constructed a backdrop of paper columns representing the original Washington, DC, setting. The singing of an appropriate freedom song may precede this choral dramatization.

On the back wall there is a large photo or drawing of the Rev. Dr. Martin Luther King Jr. Also on back wall there is a large paper or cloth "Collage of Brotherhood" created by the class. Numbers 6–10 form the horizontal line, and Numbers 1–5 form a line in front of them. The rest of the class forms two even clusters on either side of the horizontal lines. There is a small table and three chairs downstage.

Number 1: *(Steps forward.)* I say to you today, my friends, that in spite of the difficulties and frustrations of the moment, I still have a dream . . .

Number 2: *(Steps forward.)* I still have a dream . . .

Number 3: *(Steps forward.)* I still have a dream . . .

Number 4: *(Steps forward.)* I still have a dream . . .

Number 5: *(Steps forward.)* It is a dream deeply rooted in the American dream. I have a dream that one day this nation will rise up and live out the true meaning of its creed.

ALL: We hold these truths to be self-evident that all . . . are created equal.

Number 6: I have a dream that one day in the red hills of Georgia, the sons of former slaves, and the sons of former slave holders will be able to sit down at the table of brotherhood . . . *(Numbers 6–10 take the cloth "Collage of Brotherhood," spread it on the table downstage, and mime sharing and eating.)*

Number 1: I have a dream that . . . little children will one day live in a nation where they will not be judged by the color of their skin but by the content of their character.

ALL: We have a dream today.

Number 7: *(Group A pantomimes as the following line is said.)* I have a dream that one day every valley shall be exalted . . . *(Group holds hands and* lowers itself in slow motion), every hill and mountain shall be made low (Group makes jagged angles with hands and arms, then slowly straightens out into original lines—making a beautiful flowing soft sound), and the rough places (Group contorts bodies) will be made plain (Group slowly holds up clasped hands) and the crooked places will be made straight.

Number 8: (Group B makes an outline of mimed mountain to the following) This is our hope ... with this faith we will be able to hew out of the mountain of despair, a stone of hope ... (Rest of cast makes discordant sounds)

Number 4: With this faith we will be able to transform the jangling discords of our nation ... (Discordant sounds cease) into a beautiful symphony of brotherhood. (The cast joins hands)

Number 9: (Group C pantomimes to the following) With this faith we will be able to work together (Group mimes work, farming, office, or sports) ... pray together, struggle together (Group makes proud, straight line).

Number 10: Stand up for freedom together ...

Number 3: Knowing that we will be free one day ...

ALL: Let freedom ring ... (Cast forms two lines as in a triangular bell)

Number 5: Let freedom ring.

Number 2: This will be the day ... when all of God's children will be able to sing with new meaning:

ALL: (Sing) My country, 'tis of thee, sweet land of liberty, of thee I sing. Land where my fathers died, land of the Pilgrims' pride, from every mountainside, let freedom ring.

Number 8: Let freedom ring from every hill and molehill ...

Number 7: From every mountain top, let freedom ring!

Number 6: And when this happens, when we allow freedom to ring—when we let it ring from every village and every hamlet, from every city ...

Number 1 and Number 10: We will be able to speed up that day when all of God's children, Black ... and White ... Jews ... and Gentiles, Protestants, and Catholics (All join hands or shake hands) ... will be able to join hands and sing in the words of the Negro spiritual. (Two lines blend in a semicircle.)

ALL: Free at last, thank God Almighty, we are free at last! (All raise clasped hands into the air.)

We Still Have a Dream: From Page to Stage (Grades 3–6)

Dramatization of the "I Have a Dream" speech by Dr. Martin Luther King Jr.

The following lesson sequence covers three to five days, two periods a day. Feel free to adjust and rearrange the schedule to best fit the needs of you and your class.

Act Out the Speech

Sessions 1 and 2

Goal: Students will present parts of Dr. King's "I Have a Dream" speech in a creative way.

Materials: Several poster boards, Magic Markers, tape recorder, copies of "We Still Have a Dream" adaptation; if possible, a recording of Dr. King's speech.

Warm-Up: Make a Peace Web

1. Ask students to form circles consisting of five or six players each.

2. Direct them to close their eyes, extend their arms forward, and move slowly and silently forward to the center of the circle.

3. Make sure that they understand that each of their hands must gently grasp and hold on to another hand of someone else in the group. Coach, "Keep your eyes closed. Make sure that each of your hands is gently holding on to one other hand of a teammate in your group." Coach the students to make a soft humming sound. They have now created a beautiful "peace web," which will be integrated into the "We Still Have a Dream" dramatization.

Please note: If students cannot absolutely untangle themselves, emphasize that coming as far as they did making the web was an accomplishment in itself. They stuck with the problem and gave it their all making the web.

Teamwork works—students and teachers make peace links to honor Dr. Martin Luther King Jr. (Photo: Sally Ann Milgrim)

Help them understand that sometimes the "yarn" gets so tangled into a knot that it is impossible to untie. To have some fun, a giant human scissors can be formed by a small group to "cut through" the ball of yarn. In any case, if the students reach an impasse untangling the web, they all should rightfully salute their efforts for trying.

Development

1. Ask students, "Have you ever looked forward to a day in your life in which you were expecting something important to happen? How did that make you feel? Why?" Explain that today they will be reenacting an event thousands of people had looked forward to attending.

2. Discuss with students the circumstances leading to the "March on Washington for Jobs and Freedom," held on August 25, 1963.

3. Help them create the mood of that day by inviting them to imagine they are at the march on a bright, warm summer's day;

250,000 people are gathered in front of the Lincoln Memorial. Students, on the spot, can interview people there from all walks of life. Provide resource materials or have older students research the events leading to the march and the day of the march. For example, singers Harry Belafonte and Mahalia Jackson might be interviewed about the songs they will sing today. People coming off the bus from Wisconsin, Texas, or another state might be interviewed—people of all different ages, religions, and color.

Focus on Content

4. Guide students to interview Dr. King before he speaks. (Students work in pairs or in small groups.) Dr. King intends to talk about the unfulfilled promises of this country regarding civil rights since Lincoln's Emancipation Proclamation, 100 years ago.

Wrap-Up

What kind of a day is it? What is the mood of the throng? What are the expectations regarding Dr. King's speech?

Extensions and Enrichments

Guide students to think about a character to play during Days 3–5. They should follow these basic guidelines and research details: "Who am I? What does my character want? Why is my character at the March? How does he or she speak?"

Session 3

Goal: Students will create a bond of friendship in movement and song.

Materials: Song sheets of freedom songs: "Oh, Freedom," "We Shall Not Be Moved," and "We Shall Overcome."

Warm-Up

Coach the students to make a peace web (see pp. 158–160).

Development

1. Form a circle of friendship. Guide students to form a circle, hold hands, and imagine that "friendship electricity" is running through the circle, giving all kinds of positive energy. They can hum together softly as the electricity moves around the circle.

2. Guide students to create a peace web. Maintaining circle formation, students hold hands. Direct them to close their eyes, extend one arm forward, and move slowly toward the center of the circle. Each student gently grasps and holds on to the hand of another student. The resulting configuration should look like a giant ball of yarn. The group slowly unwinds, humming the song "Oh, Freedom."

3. Sing freedom songs. The group can keep its circle or form another comfortable configuration.

"Oh, Freedom"

Oh, freedom
Oh, freedom
Oh, freedom over me . . .
And before I'll be a slave,
I'll be buried in my grave,
And go home to my Lord and be free.

"We Shall Not Be Moved!"

We shall not
We shall not be moved . . .
We shall not
We shall not be moved . . .
Just like a tree that's
Standing by the water
We shall not be moved!

> Black and White together
> We shall not be moved,
> Just like a tree that's
> Standing by the water
> We shall not be moved!

> "We Shall Overcome"

> We shall overcome
> We shall overcome
> We shall overcome
> Some day
> Oh, deep in my heart
> I do believe
> We shall overcome
> Some day, some day.

4. Distribute choral reading script of "We Still Have a Dream" and have students take turns reading it aloud.

5. Assign the parts (Numbers 1–10). Depending on the size of your class, assign two or three students to each number.

6. Guide students to prepare a set—for example, long columns of butcher paper for the Washington Monument; "Collage of Brotherhood," pictures and words composed by players themselves; symbols, such as doves. Encourage students to come up with their own ideas.

Wrap-Up

Ask students, "Why do you think August 25, 1963, was a day of peace and harmony? How did people express their hopes for freedom and peace?"

Extensions and Enrichments

Instruct students to look over parts for next day's presentation and review the script several times with partners.

Sessions 4 and 5

Goal: Students will present a choral reading of "We Still Have a Dream."

Materials: Scripts of "We Still Have a Dream."

Warm-Up

Coach students to make a peace web (see pp. 158–160).

Development

1. Guide students to practice choral reading with assigned parts. Make sure that they speak clearly and with feeling in unison during choral parts with proper emphasis of words.

2. Guide them to integrate pantomime with words. For example, in group pantomime, for the image of "jangling discords of our nation," players form jagged angles with hands and arms at oblique angles with a variety of standing, sitting, and squatting positions, creating an image of disharmony; for "mountain of despair," a group makes outline of asymmetrical mountain, mirrors each other (see p. 39), adds soft sounds, and joins together as "stones of hope." For the image of "a beautiful symphony of brotherhood," players form a "band of brotherhood," holding hands and making soft sounds.

Focus on Content

3. Guide students to explore individual pantomime opportunities, such as making a "symphony of brotherhood": Americans at work and at play, all done in mime (farmer hoeing land, planting crops; office workers using computers; letter carriers, doctors, athletes, and so on, in characteristic action poses).

---

4. Integrate music and sounds; for example, for "symphony of brotherhood," make a "sound collage" (see Sounds in Harmony, p. 28).

5. Pay attention that transformation from one mimed image into another is smooth or in slow motion with appropriate sounds and music.

6. Guide students to perform the choral reading after several run-throughs. Some students can play marchers. A hush falls over the crowd. Dr. King abandons his prepared text, which he had spent most of the previous night writing, and "We Still Have a Dream" is dramatically recited by the group.

Wrap-Up

1. Discuss with students what happened after Dr. King delivered his speech. Guide students, after researching the march, to conduct, in role, interviews at the White House with other civil rights leaders and President Kennedy. Newspaper people the world over heralded the speech. One British journalist called it "the most moving and magnificent public address I have ever heard."

2. Discuss how the March on Washington and Dr. King's stirring words spurred on the Civil Rights Act of 1964 and the Voting Rights Act of 1965.

3. Engage students to discuss and share their vision of what Dr. King's world could look like. Ask them to express the dreams they have for themselves, for their school, for their neighborhood, and beyond. Encourage them to give examples of how they would begin to make their dreams come alive.

Extensions and Enrichments

- Students can create works of art, music, drama, and writing to extend their visions of living in a peaceful world.

Manhattan students enact Dr. Martin Luther King Jr.'s receiving the Nobel Peace Prize. (Photo: Steve Denes)

Dramatizing Poetry (Grades 3–6)

From "I Dream a World" by Langston Hughes.

Ask your students, "What dreams do you have? How can you follow and keep them close to you?"

> I dream a world where man
> No other man will scorn,
> Where love will bless the earth
> And peace its path adorn.
> I dream a world where all
> Will know sweet freedom's way . . .

Act Out the Poem

Goal: Students will act out the Langston Hughes poem segment and their own poetry through interrelating them in theme, sound, and movement.

Materials: The Langston Hughes poem and student poems.

Warm-Up

Ask the students to write out their deeply felt dreams for a better world—for themselves and for others. Call on volunteers to read aloud their dreams for a better world.

Development

Goal: Students act out the Langston Hughes poem segment and their own poetry by interrelating them in theme, sound, and movement.

Materials: The Langston Hughes poem segment and student poems.

1. Read the poems aloud with student readers.

2. Discuss with students their feelings about the poems. Ask them such questions as "How do you think the poems are related? What are your favorite images in the poems? What do you think each poem is trying to say?"

3. Divide the class into two groups: one, from "I Dream a World," and two, students' own poetry.

4. Guide each group to come up with sounds (including the words of the poem itself) and movement that will best express the essence of what they think the Hughes poem and the student poems in Group 2 are expressing.

5. Guide the class to interweave the two groups in sound and movement. This process can take the form of mixing sounds of the poems, the poems alternating, or the poems recited in a straightforward progression.

6. Experiment, experiment, experiment!

7. Present the poems/play/production in the class and then invite another class to hear and see the presentation.

> ### Focus on Content
>
> ## Wrap-Up
>
> - Conduct a discussion on enacting the poetry. Ask, "What worked well? Can you give some examples? What needed work? Examples? Would the students do the presentation differently by adding, deleting, or changing anything specific?" Invite them to make the changes and perform the presentation again.

Extensions and Enrichments

- Encourage students to make copies of the two poems and illustrate them.

- Suggest that they write poems expressing their own dreams.

- Guide them to create a collage or mural of their own poetry.

And so our peaceful journey now comes to a close. But, of course, we know there will be many more for you and your students as you try these enactments of stories and varied exercises—and as you add your own enriching variations. We wish you and your students many more delightful experiences as you continue your peaceful journeys filled with positive classroom spirit.

Helpful Resources

Alexander, Lloyd. (1990). *The big book for peace*. New York: E. P. Dutton Children's Books.
Coerr, Elinor. (1977). *Sadako and the thousand cranes*. New York: Putnam.
Courlander, Harold. (1959). The tiger's whisker. In *The tiger's whisker and other tales and legend from Asia and the Pacific*. New York: Harcourt Brace Jovanovich.

Cowley, Joy. (1969). *The duck in the gun.* New York: Doubleday.

Fine, Esther Sokolov, Lacey, Ann, & Baer, Joan. (1995). *Children as peacemakers.* Portsmouth, NH: Heinemann.

Hayes, Jennifer Fell, & Schindel, Dorothy Napp. (1994). *Pioneer journeys: Drama in museum education.* Charlottesville, VA: New Plays.

MacDonald, Margaret Reed. (2005). *Peace tales: World tales to talk about.* Little Rock, AR: August House.

National Gallery of Art. http://www.nga.gov/search/index.shtm. For color pictures of the *Peaceable Kingdom* (1834) by Edward Hicks as well as images taken from the painting.

Severn, Bill. (1959). *Shadow magic: The story of shadow play.* New York: David McKay.

ABOUT THE AUTHORS

Milton E. Polsky has taught creative drama at New York City public schools and at New York University, the City University of New York, and Hofstra University. He is the author of numerous books and articles on the values and uses of drama in the classroom and beyond. He is currently the cochair of the UFT Players (United Federation of Teachers), an organization that has produced many of his plays. Dr. Polsky is a recipient of the Rod Marriott Award for Outstanding Lifetime Achievement in Theatre Education, presented by the New York State Theatre Education Association. With his wife, Roberta, he lives in New York City, where his children Jonah and Maddy also reside.

Dorothy Napp Schindel is the director of DramaMUSE Associates, a company that creates interactive theater and drama-based programs for museums. Her book *Pioneer Journeys: Drama in Museum Education* (coauthored with Jennifer Fell Hayes) is a recipient of the American Alliance for Theatre and Education's Distinguished Book Award. A director, scenic designer, and educational theater specialist, she has taught at all levels, from kindergarten through college, and has worked in regional and off-Broadway theaters. Ms. Schindel, a native New Yorker and mother of Deanna and Emily, is author of many articles and presenter and board member for numerous professional organizations. She and her husband Stephen reside in Vero Beach, Florida, and Becket, Massachusetts.

ABOUT THE AUTHORS

Carmine Tabone is the director of the Jersey City–based Educational Arts Team and an adjunct faculty member at New York University in the Educational Theatre Program. He has served as a board member of the American Alliance for Theatre and Education and as a regional governor for the Children's Theatre Association of America. Tabone has conducted hundreds of workshops—in schools, libraries, and churches and at regional, national, and international conferences—and he has coauthored articles on the uses of theater arts in educational settings. He lives in New Jersey with his wife, Laura; his son and daughter, Matt and Sara; and Houdini, his dog.